Praise for *Teaching to Empower*

More than ever, education leaders must reconcile archaic thinking when addressing the needs of students. Zacarian and Silverstone carefully walk us through the notion that the evolution of students demands a new mindset that reflects on historical realities and cultivates courageous innovation to build future empowered minds.

—Lauren S. Ford
Senior Manager, Leadership Development, Houston ISD Educational Learning Center

This timely book will support systems as they shift paradigms toward an assets-based approach when instructing and empowering students. The collection of both research and practical strategies will assist educators as they work to meet the cultural, linguistic, and social-emotional needs of our most vulnerable students.

—Ivannia Soto
Professor of Education, Whittier College, and Bilingual Educator Strategic Training Director at the California Association for Bilingual Education

Teaching to Empower is extremely illuminating for anyone seeking sound and liberating pedagogical theories and practices. For those searching for the gained experiences of effective schools all across the country, it is indispensable. Zacarian and Silverstone show that a school can contribute to the development of citizens able to exercise empathy and solidarity. They raise key questions about the finality of schools, confront these with educators' actual duty, and give extensive examples of good school practices that lead to real change. There is no better time to read this book. It is an invitation to educators to rethink their vocation and their practice to serve a more just country.

—Ana María García Blanco
Executive Director, Instituto Nueva Escuela
Rio Piedras, Puerto Rico

High-stakes testing and the prioritization of speed of coverage over depth can distract us from connecting to the young people we teach. *Teaching to Empower* brings us back to the heart of education by giving examples and structures that help support the development of agency and social-emotional well-being in classroom communities.

—Marta Donahoe
2019 Montessori Society Living Legacy Honoree

TEACHING TO EMPOWER

DEBBIE
ZACARIAN

MICHAEL
SILVERSTONE

TEACHING TO
EMPOWER

Taking Action to Foster Student Agency, Self-Confidence, and Collaboration

ASCD

ALEXANDRIA, VIRGINIA USA

1703 N. Beauregard St. • Alexandria, VA 22311-1714 USA
Phone: 800-933-2723 or 703-578-9600 • Fax: 703-575-5400
Website: www.ascd.org • E-mail: member@ascd.org
Author guidelines: www.ascd.org/write

Ranjit Sidhu, *Executive Director and CEO;* Stefani Roth, *Publisher;* Genny Ostertag, *Director, Content Acquisitions;* Susan Hills, *Senior Acquisitions Editor;* Julie Houtz, *Director, Book Editing & Production;* Katie Martin, *Editor;* Judi Connelly, *Senior Art Director;* Donald Ely, *Associate Art Director;* Circle Graphics, *Typesetter;* Kelly Marshall, *Interim Manager, Production Services;* Trinay Blake, *E-Publishing Specialist;* Tristan Coffelt, *Senior Production Specialist*

All web links in this book are correct as of the publication date below but may have become inactive or otherwise modified since that time. If you notice a deactivated or changed link, please e-mail books@ascd.org with the words "Link Update" in the subject line. In your message, please specify the web link, the book title, and the page number on which the link appears.

PAPERBACK ISBN: 978-1-4166-2854-5   ASCD product #120006   n3/20
PDF E-BOOK ISBN: 978-1-4166-2856-9; see Books in Print for other formats.

Quantity discounts are available: e-mail programteam@ascd.org or call 800-933-2723, ext. 5773, or 703-575-5773. For desk copies, go to www.ascd.org/deskcopy.

Library of Congress Cataloging-in-Publication Data

Names: Zacarian, Debbie, author. | Silverstone, Michael (Elementary teacher), author.
Title: Teaching to empower : taking action to foster student agency, self-confidence, and collaboration / Debbie Zacarian, Michael Silverstone.
Description: Alexandria, Virginia USA : ASCD, [2020] | Includes bibliographical references and index.
Identifiers: LCCN 2019048630 (print) | LCCN 2019048631 (ebook) | ISBN 9781416628545 (paperback) | ISBN 9781416628569 (pdf)
Subjects: LCSH: Motivation in education. | Classroom environment. | Teacher-student relationships.
Classification: LCC LB1065 .Z34 2020 (print) | LCC LB1065 (ebook) | DDC 370.154—dc23
LC record available at https://lccn.loc.gov/2019048630
LC ebook record available at https://lccn.loc.gov/2019048631

29 28 27 26 25 24 23 22 21 20   1 2 3 4 5 6 7 8 9 10 11 12

TEACHING TO EMPOWER

Introduction

As educators, we are charged with continually adopting and adapting new curricula while doing our best to ensure that students develop and can apply the skills they will need in school and beyond. Educators' work must also take into account long-standing structural inequalities and our biases, both of which can foil even the best-intentioned efforts to provide the type of empowering education that prepares students to succeed in dynamic, collaborative working environments where cooperation, self-direction, self-reliance, communication, and interdependence are the norm.

We must also be keenly aware of the ever-changing demographics in our student and family populations and the need to build better, stronger, and more meaningful relationships with students based on who they are personally, culturally, socially, economically, and academically. The urgency of making these connections and being more responsive to student needs is underscored by the disparity of graduation rates among students of different demographic groups. Indeed, data provided by the National Center for Education Statistics (2015, 2016, 2017) show clear and unacceptable patterns of inequitable outcomes (see Figure A).

These outcomes suggest that such students are operating from a disadvantage that schools and society are still failing to address. What makes this a particularly urgent and complicated challenge is that, while student and family populations are diversifying, educators remain a fairly homogenous workforce (Musu-Gillette et al., 2016; U.S. Department of Education, 2016). Consider these facts:

- Suburban U.S. schools are seeing rapid growth and dynamic changes in students and families from culturally, economically, linguistically, and racially diverse populations (Edwards, Domke, & White, 2017).

FIGURE A

Graduation Rates of U.S. Students by Subgroup, 2014–2017

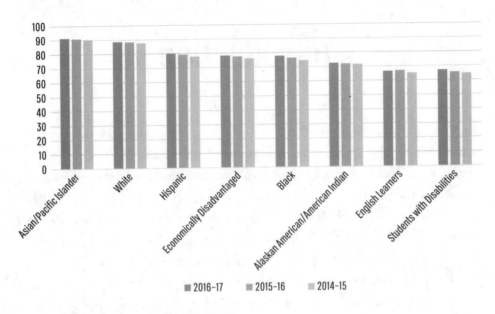

Source: National Center for Education Statistics, 2016, 2017, 2018.

- While schools in high-poverty and urban areas employ a more diverse group of teachers, the overwhelming percentage of U.S. school principals and teachers are white (U.S. Department of Education, 2016).
- A startling 51 percent of students in the United States live in poverty (Southern Education Foundation, 2015).
- English learners are one of the fastest-growing groups across the United States (National Center for Education Statistics, 2019a).
- More than half of U.S. students have experienced or are experiencing significant childhood adversity (National Center for Health Statistics, 2013).

Given the dynamic changes that are continuously occurring in U.S. society, including the rapid growth of nonwhite populations (Humes, Jones, & Ramirez, 2011), and given the evolving skill demands that educators will be expected to address, what is the way forward? How is it possible for us to foster the resilience, persistence, self-direction, cultural and social responsiveness, and collaboration that students will need to navigate the complexities of the future? How can we best serve a diverse population? What does an effective education really look like today, and what might it look like in the future?

We'd like to share two classroom experiences that have informed our response to these questions and helped shape our vision of education that prioritizes the development and use of student voice. In the first example, one half of our author team, Michael, observed 2nd grade students developing their voices quite literally while learning to sing as a group. Here are his reflections on what he saw:

> If you've never done it, it's very tricky to learn to sing a round. Even a song as simple as "Row, Row, Row Your Boat" requires a child to remember the words, the pitch, the rhythm, and to somehow hear it inside and get their voices to sing it out with confidence into the air. For many adults, it would be a breakthrough to simply do that.
>
> But there's a second part of learning to sing a round that is equally important—to listen, to understand what is happening around you and find a way to precisely respond to that without losing track of your part while still being mindful of what you're hearing. . . .
>
> Music can be a model of what it feels like when the voice within joins skillfully with the community. It promotes a sense of well-being. Because it is rhythmic and communal, it creates a shared framework that individuals can feel aware of while also maintaining an awareness of their own spirit. They can feel the support and reassuring guidance of being part of some intelligent endeavor that is larger than the self. (Silverstone, 2017, paras. 1–2, 10)

Encapsulated here is a model that presents learning as developing and refining two different kinds of awareness simultaneously. There is the internal awareness of oneself—one's ideas, talents, perspective, and impulses (what each of us sings), and then there is the external awareness of what is happening around us—what others are doing, and where we might fit in with them and make our useful contribution without losing connection to ourselves or taking away from others (fitting our voice into the sound the group is making). Without both kinds of awareness, learning is incomplete. Absolutely, students need experiences that allow them to discover and follow their individual ideas, impulses, preferences, talents, and perspectives. It's just as important, though, that they also learn to attend with precision to what is happening around them and how they might serve, with thoughtfulness and care, the needs of their peers, their classroom, their community, their society, and, ultimately, their world.

Debbie, the other half of our author team, also had an experience that illustrates the potential of self-reliance and effective personal capacity that all students possess and that educators might do more to cultivate:

> Early in my first years in public education, when I was working with a high school student whose mother was terminally ill, I got a call from that student's father. "Hi, Debbie," he said. "This is Mary's dad. My wife just died. Can you tell Mary and then bring her to the hospital so that she can say goodbye to her mom?"
>
> I worried about how to tell Mary in a way that would be sensitive and supportive. I remember gently sharing with her the news that she had known was imminent and then driving her to the hospital. When we arrived, Mary hugged her mom for a while and then broke away to greet the hospital staff and thank them, by name, for the care that they had provided her mother, father, and her. I remember how her actions were so surprising to me. Surprising because she had such grace, gratitude, and composure at the early age of 15 and could engage in these spontaneous, mature, and self-initiated conversations at such a moment of loss.
>
> It was an experience that stayed with me, and one that I often come back to with questions: What was it that fueled Mary to express her gratitude in such a powerful way? Was this an ability that she had developed on her own? Had she learned it from her mom? Her dad? Her friends? Teachers? All of us together? It is these questions that drive me to think about what it would take for more of our students to build these capacities. What would it take for them—even those who, like Mary, had endured or were enduring trauma—to feel safe enough to express their true selves, to feel empathetic toward others, and to feel competent and confident in what they say and what they do?

The education that many of us received emphasized following and being led. In a time of change, when information is widely available to anyone with the skills to understand and organize it, we need a new model of teaching and learning that provides students with skills for self-direction and collaboration. These are the skills that will help them be effective citizens when finding a way forward requires active negotiation.

Our book is designed to support educators' efforts to create a culture of empowerment, collaboration, and initiative that will help *all* students—inclusive of race, culture, language, background, socioeconomic status, abilities, sexuality, or gender— grow into active learners, active community members, and engaged global citizens. Undergirding our thinking is the belief that every student deserves to experience meaningful and practical learning opportunities and supportive apprenticeships with teachers and others. In the pages ahead, we will lead pre- and in-service teachers to reflect on the historical roots of educational empowerment, describe what an empowered student looks like in increasingly diverse contemporary schools, and explore what educators' own relationship to empowerment is. We will also provide guidance on

- Creating inclusive and empowering physical learning spaces;
- Setting up self-directed learning and positive interdependence;
- Promoting student self-reflection;
- Teaching the skills of collaboration;
- Helping students develop the skills of self-advocacy that they need to engage in deeper, more autonomous learning; and
- Partnering with families and the community to support student empowerment.

Each chapter includes evidence-based principles and practices, protocols, and authentic K–12 examples. We draw from the wisdom of inspiring colleagues from across the continental United States and Puerto Rico who possess the confidence and determination to continually experiment to meet the dynamic needs of their students. For us, these educators are models of exactly what we hope all students will become: self-directed lifelong learners with a voice in their work, a strong and responsive connection to their community, and a meaningful role in contributing to a better world.

In this spirit, we begin by exploring the following question: *What does an empowered student look like?*

What Does an Empowered Student Look Like?

When we provide professional development and ask teachers to describe what an empowered student looks like, they often offer the examples of heroic young people like Malala Yousafzai and Emma Gonzalez, both of whom spoke up for themselves and for others, raising international awareness about the social issues and discrimination that they had faced firsthand.

Both of these names are probably familiar to you. In 2012, at the age of 15, Malala Yousafzai survived an assassination attempt by a member of the Taliban in Swat Valley, Pakistan (Malala Fund, 2018). She was targeted in response to her persistent defiance of the Taliban's ban on female education. At great personal risk, Malala used social networking to let the world know what was happening under Taliban rule, and she became widely known for her relentless pursuit of girls' right to an education. At the age of 17, she became the youngest-ever recipient of the Nobel Peace Prize, recognized for her activist efforts. In February 2018, 18-year-old Emma Gonzalez sheltered with classmates in her school's auditorium during a shooting rampage at the Marjory Stoneman Douglas High School in Parkland, Florida. Just two days after the shooting, she delivered a passionate and persuasive personal statement at a gun control rally.

Subsequently, Emma helped to lead massive student and teacher walkouts in the United States and elsewhere, demanding legislative protection from gun violence.

While these two are known to millions, there are countless everyday examples of students in our classrooms who have taken stands for themselves and their own right to self-determination, for their classmates and communities, and for what they feel is right. In this chapter, we explore the interconnected attributes of empowered students—their habits, traits, and mindsets—and examine how these attributes support positive outcomes in their learning and beyond. We'll do this by considering the following topics, for the following reasons:

- **The dynamically changing definition of an empowered student.** Historical context sheds important light on our current practices and values.
- **Critical factors in diverse classroom contexts.** These factors must guide how we tailor education practice to serve changing student populations.
- **Preconditions for student empowerment.** These set the stage for successful autonomous and collaborative learning.
- **The intersection of personal responsibility and social interaction.** Exploring this topic clarifies how students can share responsibility for creating a safe and empathetic community focused on the greater good.
- **Empowerment through adaptation.** Our students must be able to successfully respond to ever-changing environments.

Student empowerment is a complex concept that has evolved over time. To understand it more thoroughly, we need to grasp both its historical meaning and its current definition and application in contemporary education. A first step toward taking action to help all our students to be empowered is to explore what we mean by *an empowered student*.

The Dynamically Changing Definition of an Empowered Student

Let's dig a little deeper into why Malala Yousafzai and Emma Gonzalez might so frequently be offered as examples of empowered students. We would argue that their empowerment is rooted in two factors: personal action and collective responsibility. Both of these young women seized opportunities to gain a sense of control and assert agency in decisions that affected their lives. They took initiative, acting with confidence and autonomy. Drawing on personal experience, they identified a collective need in the public sphere. They bore responsibility and made contributions to a collective good.

While Malala Yousafzai and Emma Gonzalez are singularly dramatic examples of empowered students, all students possess the potential to take ownership of their own learning and choices by applying the skills and knowledge that they have acquired through personal experience (Gauvain, 2001, 2013; Rogoff, 2003). This can take many forms, such as deciding what independent study to undertake, raising a hand to state an opinion, seeking help, asking questions, and expressing needs. Each of these are examples of actions students take when they feel able to exercise their own agency in their particular situation.

The examples of Malala and Emma clearly illustrate how empowerment is commonly seen today as a combination of autonomy and collaboration. This is something of a departure from past views. The student's traditional role has been obediently following a set of explicit and implicit expectations, rules, and directives handed down by authorities. Present-day examples include high school students following a school schedule that's controlled to the minute, completing assigned and monitored tasks, and participating in mandatory examinations. Expectations like these date from the early days of a universal public education, the point of which was to help all students acquire the skills and dispositions necessary to promote the acquisition of knowledge and involved citizenry (Alexander & Alexander, 2011; Labaree, 2011).

Underlying the foundation of a universal education was the assumption that children were empty vessels who would receive the knowledge, attitudes, and moral leanings presented to them by teachers, who acted as stand-ins for their parents and religious authorities. Indeed, when public schools began in the United States in the 1800s, they reflected an uncritical and unwavering English Protestant doctrine, with moral lessons embedded in the curriculum. Consider these reading exercises from *McGuffey's Eclectic Reader*, the most common school textbook of the 19th century:

> 12. When Ralph found that he could not have the white rose, he began to scream, and snatched it. But he was soon very sorry. The thorns tore his hand. It was so sore he could not use it for some time.

13. Ralph did not soon forget this. When he wanted what he should not have, his mother would point to his sore hand. He at last learned to do as he was told. (McGuffey, 1879)

In those days, students were expected to learn through "quiet attention, obedience to teachers, and recalling and repeating material" (Cohen, 1988, p. 12). They would have been expected to exhibit the characteristics listed in Figure 1.1, because those were the attributes that they would need to achieve those goals.

FIGURE 1.1

Descriptors of Virtuous Students in 19th Century Classrooms

Acquiescent	Dutiful	Reverential
Adherent	Obedient	Submissive
Compliant	Observant	Subservient
Deferential	Passive	Unquestioning
Docile	Respectful	

It was in the first half of the 20th century that our contemporary sense of an empowered student took root. Educational scholar and reformer John Dewey advocated for a revolutionary model of education, proposing that a public school enterprise should be a place of vision, discovery, intellectual challenge, adventure, and excitement—a place where "all individuals have the opportunity to contribute something, and in which the activities in which all participate are the chief carrier of control" (Dewey, 1938, p. 56). This dramatic shift to learning by doing rather than learning through a lecture model called for cooperative classrooms where teachers would limit or reduce their all-knowing authority and elevate students' contributions as highly valuable and necessary to promote the ideals of social responsibility in a democracy.

Following this train of thought, if we use Dewey's thinking to guide our thinking about the characteristics of an empowered student, we wind up with a very different set of descriptors (see Figure 1.2).

FIGURE 1.2

Descriptors of Collaborative Students in Post-Dewey Classrooms

Adaptable	Energetic	Insightful	Perseverant
Artistic	Experimental	Intuitive	Problem-solving
Collaborative	Extroverted	Knowledgeable	Resilient
Committed	Flexible	Loyal	Respectful
Courageous	Generous	Mindful	Self-controlled
Confident (or self-confident)	Honest	Nonjudgmental	Validating
	Honorable	Observant	Valued
Creative	Humble	Open-minded	Witty
Daring	Humorous	Outspoken	
Determined	Industrious	Passionate	

Among the terms in Figure 1.2 are several that earlier generations of educators would recognize as student virtues. But notice how many skew active rather than passive and how many seem collaborative and creative rather than receptive. It is not that the post-Dewey shift in philosophy completely abandoned the norms or mission of the past; the teaching profession simply expanded its definition of empowerment to be broader and more complex.

 Time for Reflection

1. Which of the words in Figure 1.2 would you use to describe an empowered student? Before you circle your choices, think about how each characteristic might factor into autonomous learning and collaborative pursuit of a group goal.
2. Now look back to Figure 1.1 and circle the words there that describe an empowered student. What type of overlap do you note in the words you circled in both figures?

When we (Debbie and Michael) completed this reflection task, we found that many words from both lists fit our concept of an empowered student, among them *observant* and *respectful* (i.e., students who can learn effectively from seeing models and are considerate of the needs of others) from the first list and *adaptable, daring, flexible, mindful,* and *open-minded* from the second. This collection of terms illustrates how the phrase *empowered student* represents a paradox in contemporary education. Today's students are expected to be autonomous yet collaborative, and they are to make the most of their individual contributions toward the common good while also working within the explicit and implied rules set forth by their learning communities.

Critical Factors in Diverse Classroom Contexts

Before going any further, we must acknowledge the long-standing barriers to empowerment that many students face. Prior to the landmark *Brown v. Board of Education* U.S. Supreme Court ruling in 1954, a K–12 public school education was not applied equally and equitably across minority and underrepresented populations; it was mostly for white Americans (Flores, 2017).

The 1960s marked a major shift in educational practices to address entrenched inequities. President Lyndon Johnson began what he called a War on Poverty, and his administration implemented the 1965 Elementary and Secondary Education Act, which earmarked funds to better serve students from poor and underrepresented communities (Stone, 2009). Many seminal Supreme Court cases were brought forth during the 1960s to address the inequality experienced by the nation's students who were poor, nonwhite, non-native English speakers, and homeless, as well as students with disabilities (Alexander & Alexander, 2011; Stanford University, n.d.). In his research on social recognition, Peter Gabel (2018), a public interest lawyer and theorist, describes these unification efforts as transformative toward the mutually agreed-upon societal shift toward social justice and equity in the United States. They signaled a new role for student empowerment and an elevated responsibility for attending to it.

Across U.S. rural, suburban, and urban communities, the school-age population continues to diversify, and with this shift has come a good deal of research documenting the value of student collaboration. Almost 100 years after Dewey's philosophical contributions on the importance of students' contributions, we have significant scientific evidence showing cooperative learning to be an invaluable method of supporting autonomous learning and citizenry in a democratic society. It is especially effective in diverse student populations (Cohen & Lotan, 2014). However, a teacher limiting his or her direct authority and giving students cooperative learning tasks is no guarantee that students will take the initiative and assume responsibility for their learning, let alone the responsibility of supporting their peers' efforts to learn. Students' success in cooperative learning environments depends on an array of factors involving the skills and agreements that allow for autonomy and collaboration. An essential one is students' perceptions of their own status as well as the status of others (Cohen & Lotan, 2014).

Social psychologist Claude Steele (2010) researched a phenomenon called *stereotype threat,* which is what certain groups of students can feel when they perceive themselves to be in an ethnic, racial, cultural, economic, or gender group that is not expected to show mastery or success. Steele found that, without intervention, stereotype threat has a significantly negative effect on student outcomes. Given this finding, it's educators' responsibility to intervene—to intentionally provide a certain set of conditions that disrupt stereotype threat and promote student empowerment. According to Steele, when students perceive themselves or others as largely incapable of being successful in school, this prediction is likely to become self-fulfilling. Conversely, the internalized attitudes associated with being in a group that is expected to experience success can make that outcome more likely.

Let's pause to consider an example of two 5-year-old students preparing for their first public school experience. Dyana is the daughter of migrant farm workers, and she has grown up watching her parents plant and harvest fruits and vegetables. The family lives sometimes in housing furnished by the owners of the land they work, and sometimes in whatever other housing they can afford (including, occasionally, their car). While Dyana was born in the United States and is a citizen, her parents are undocumented, and she has grown up observing their uneasiness and fear of deportation. Now, at age 5, she is increasingly aware of their tenuous situation even though she is still too young to fully understand its meaning. In public, she has learned to make herself quiet and unobtrusive, as her parents do.

Suzanne is a kindergarten classmate of Dyana's. Her parents own and operate a local store and have branched out to include quite a few franchises in their professional real estate portfolio. Both of Suzanne's parents have advanced degrees in accounting, and the family lives in a large, beautiful home in a wealthy section of town. Suzanne thrived in preschool, and her parents encourage behaviors in their daughter that they expect will be valued in her kindergarten classroom: be curious, be adventurous, listen to the teacher, try hard, and follow the rules but also your interests. They want Suzanne to experience the kind of success that they did as students.

We provide this example as a reminder of a few of the ways that circumstances can contribute to some students coming to school as tentative learners and others as confident ones. The stereotype threat that Steele (2010) and developmental psychologist and social scientist Roseanne L. Flores (2017) describe (and that Dyana and Suzanne are experiencing) is epitomized in a *Forbes* article titled "How the Rich Raise Their Kids" (Moyer, 2007). The article shows the sweeping differences between wealthy and poor families, particularly in expectations and perceptions. For example, the expectation of children being reared by wealthy parents or guardians is that they will attend college; these families have ample access and resources, and they rarely consider the possibility of an alternative. Conversely, children of poor and working-class families are described as living in a survival-oriented world reminiscent of the one in the dystopian young adult novel *The Hunger Games;* only a small percentage have the opportunity to attend college, and the majority try to succeed by graduating from high school into a working world where fewer and fewer jobs offer the promise of economic security, homeownership, and health care.

While some people may consider this an overly dramatic comparison, what is beyond question is that too many students lack the opportunities they need and deserve to achieve empowerment. That's where educators must step in.

 Time for Reflection

1. What additional examples can you provide of the types of diversity you have encountered as a student or as an educator? These might include differences

in language, race, ethnicity, gender, sexuality, and other factors among the students or educators with whom you have worked or learned.

2. How have your experiences with diversity affected your attitudes about differences among learners or among colleagues?

3. Consider some common types of racial, ethnic, cultural, gender, or other forms of diversity in the general population that you have had little or no experience with as a student or as an educator. How might this lack of exposure have influenced the formation of your attitudes about people from these populations?

4. What are some beliefs you hold about the difference in educational experiences between wealthy families and working-class and less privileged families?

The Intersection of Personal Responsibility and Social Interaction

An additional strand of our construct of student empowerment is social responsibility toward fellow community members and the intention to serve a greater good.

Let's look at an example of what we mean by social responsibility. A class of 4th grade students is on a field trip, taking a group hike up a mountain trail as part of their study of geological rock formations. One student, Devin, lags behind the rest. Two of Devin's classmates, Jackie and Louie, decide on their own—that is, autonomously—to walk back down the trail to where Devin has paused to catch his breath. Without any prompting from their teacher, the two accompany Devin the rest of the way to the summit. We overhear their exchange:

> **Devin:** I'm totally out of breath.
> **Jackie:** We got you.
> **Louie:** Yeah, I had to catch my breath, too.
> **Jackie:** Don't worry; we'll take our time and get there together.

These words of mutual support are expressions of how students can share the responsibility of creating a safe and empathetic learning community. These are quieter versions of the public courage and character embodied by empowered student leaders like Malala Yousafzai and Emma Gonzalez.

To take such actions, students must have a good deal of awareness and the capacity to pick up the verbal and nonverbal messages others are sending. Take, for example, what Jackie and Louie saw when they observed Devin, before any words had been exchanged. They saw a classmate lagging behind. They realized he was struggling. They actively demonstrated their sense of care for and fellowship with Devin.

It's fair to say that practicing social responsibility begins with awareness—with paying careful attention to others. These skills do not come naturally to all students and may need to be encouraged or explicitly taught and practiced. Teachers can model such skills by being empathetic with students and seeking to identify personally with the situations they face. Both Jackie and Louie took actions that implied an understanding of what it must have felt like for Devin to lag behind the rest of the class. They also used the social and emotional language needed to express themselves appropriately in the situation, paying attention to Devin and responding in ways that were intended to help him feel safe, that he belonged, that he was valued, and that he was just as competent as everyone else.

As we will see in later chapters, this kind of solidarity among students is the obtainable result of the intentional cultivation of community within a school and within a classroom. Whether in the form of an elementary grade morning meeting or a secondary classroom gathering, moments when all students are seen, are heard, and have a chance to greet one another and share information about their lives, their work, their interests, and the challenges they face make a difference. Students need opportunities to experience, build, and nurture relationships.

Let's check back in with Devin and his classmates on the way to the summit. Devin initially responded to his peers nonverbally, by smiling at them to express gratitude that they had come to climb with him. Here's a look at the conversation as they continued up the trail:

> **Louie:** Wow, this is so steep!
>
> **Devin** (nodding vigorously): I am not used to doing this type of uphill hiking. I'm so slow.
>
> **Jackie:** Maybe it's better to go slow. We have more time to look around.
>
> **Devin:** I guess we do, yeah. Everybody's so far ahead now.
>
> **Louie:** They're going to wish they paced themselves.
>
> **Devin:** You guys are good pacers.
>
> **Jackie:** The best!

Here, we see Devin respond to his classmates' statements, signaling his agreement with them. We see him express his worry that others will make fun of him for being slow. He implies how grateful he is that Louie and Jackie helped him resolve his worry about the conflict he anticipated would arise from him lagging so far behind the group. Each of these actions during this small event depicts the attributes of socially responsible empowerment (see Figure 1.3).

FIGURE 1.3

Hallmarks of Socially Responsible Empowerment

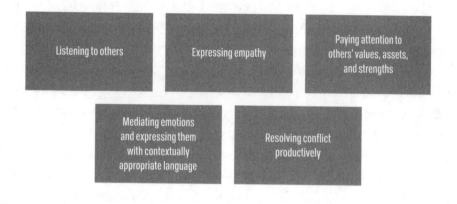

Further, the actions depicted in Figure 1.3 are what the professional literature refers to as the *social and emotional language* that students must develop (Bernard & Newell, 2013; Hertel & Johnson, 2013). We will explore instructional approaches for teaching this language in later chapters.

 Time for Reflection

1. In what ways did Jackie and Louie's words and actions demonstrate responsibility toward fellow community members and an intention of serving a greater good?

2. Consider a routine interaction among colleagues in which empathy was expressed verbally or nonverbally. What were the gestures, actions, or words that helped to convey empathy?

Empowerment Through Adaptation

Because we live in a world that is continuously changing, adaptability is a skill every-one needs. Consider how the evolution of technology requires us to learn new ways to participate in social life, access information and entertainment, navigate trans-portation, and fulfill our professional and civic responsibilities. More and more, in school contexts and beyond, students are asked to adapt to changes, large and small, as they occur. After the shooting at Emma Gonzalez's high school, for example, stu-dents there were required to exchange whatever school bag they had been carrying for bags made of see-through plastic. Whereas once school delays or cancellations were almost exclusively responses to weather conditions or building conditions, today's students might also expect disruptions in the schedule due to student or teacher walkouts and demonstrations.

A less dramatic but no less important example of a kind of adaptation that all students must master is code switching—adapting the language that they use to the circumstances in which they find themselves (DeBose, 1992; Zacarian, 2013). These fluid adaptations are needed to communicate proficiently in a variety of languages, of course, but what we are referring to here is choosing among the wide and ever-changing range of vernacular varieties spoken in diverse contexts. In the United States, these might include African American English, Chicano American English, Latin American English, and Indigenous American Vernacular English, among others (Labov, 2006; LeMoine & Soto, 2016). And there are a wide variety of regional dialect and code differences that make each of these unique and richly specific (Delpit, 1995). Within a group of high school students, the informal dialect that they use can indicate the social group to which they belong (LeMoine & Soto, 2016; Zacarian, 2013).

Let's say we observe a student talking to a friend about a school dance that they attended, and we hear one say, "Hey, bro, that be dope what you did last night." We then follow the student to his math class, where he switches to the language variety that befits the academic subject matter in response to a teacher's question: "The quadratic equation? The quadratic is a squared plus b squared equals c squared." This switch in language usage from informal (the language dialect used to express his sociocultural identity) to formal (the language used to express his academic identity) is reflective of this type of adaptability empowerment. Students must be able to adapt what they say and write to the variety of settings in which they are situated socially and academically in school and out of it. In a nutshell, empowerment through adaptability is the ability to respond effectively to changing rules and regulations within an institution, and the ability to use language deemed appropriate to different situations.

 Time for Reflection

1. Describe an additional example of empowerment through adaptability. How does your example reflect the importance of adapting to changing rules and regulations within an institution?
2. Describe an additional example of using language that is appropriate to a social context. How is it distinct from what is expected in an academic context?
3. Reflect on the different code shifts in your life—ways you use language differently or ways you exhibit different personality traits in different social contexts (e.g., at home, at work, in a public space, in a store, online).

The Interconnected Attributes of Student Empowerment

When elementary school teachers teach students about what plants need in order to grow and thrive, they share that plants need soil for nutrients, sunlight for energy, water to transport nutrients from the soil into and within the plant, and air for respiration. A teacher presenting a unit on this topic might use the illustration in Figure 1.4, featuring a giant redwood, as part of the classroom discussion.

While the presence of these four elements is essential for the growth of an individual tree, in order for it to truly thrive, it needs a fifth element: a sustainable place

FIGURE 1.4

Conditions for Growth

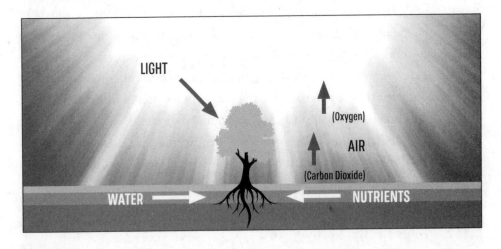

in an ecosystem. Similarly, if people are to thrive—specifically, the young people we teach—that's what they need too: a secure place in the world where they are connected to and supported by the people, systems, and ideas around them.

Empowered students, aware of these connections, exhibit the following characteristics:

1. They know institutional rules and regulations.
2. They attend to the diversity within and beyond the classroom context.
3. They are socially responsible.
4. They can adapt to dynamic changes that occur in classroom and school settings and beyond.
5. They are capable of interdependent collaboration.

Student empowerment isn't a switch that can be turned on or a state that can be achieved by inspirational slogans. It's characterized by the development and interplay of all five of these attributes. The last of these, interdependent collaboration, is particularly important but all too often overlooked. Just as plants give off life-sustaining oxygen to animals, who contribute respired carbon dioxide in return, students are part of an ecology of giving and receiving. If students are to become empowered in our schools, it will be a result of an interdependent collaboration that includes other students, educators, families, and the school community, creating an ecosystem contributing to the enrichment and satisfaction of all. As illustrated in Figure 1.5, our ultimate goal is to create an environment that supports students and gives them what they need to be contributors to a thriving and interdependent community.

FIGURE 1.5

Interconnected Attributes of Student Empowerment

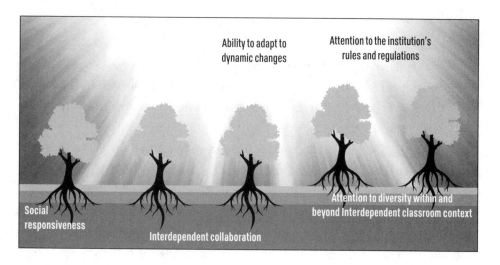

* * * * *

In the next chapter, we look more closely at how we, as teachers, can begin this process of empowerment by reflecting on our own values, understanding what drives us to be educators, and making mindful adjustments to our professional practice.

Starting with Ourselves

Fostering student empowerment is a profound purpose. Yes, we want our students to learn, but we also want them to find meaning and satisfaction in their lives. We want them to care for themselves; to care for and about others in their classroom, school, country, and global communities; and even to care for the planet itself.

In Chapter 1, we explored qualities that characterize an empowered student—namely, being (1) attentive to the institution, (2) attuned to diversity, (3) socially responsible, (4) adaptive, and (5) collaborative. As necessary as it is for students to develop and reflect these qualities, it is just as necessary for educators to model and practice them ourselves. Regardless of where we work, our particular educational role, or how long we have been educators, our most significant influence comes from our absolute willingness to take the same journey as our learners. In this chapter, we show the importance of *educators* being attentive to the institution, attuned to diversity, socially responsible, adaptive, and collaborative—and the importance of valuing these mindsets and behaviors. We will look at the skills involved and how to refine them over time to best model empowerment.

Here are the questions we will explore, and why these questions are significant:

- **What motivates an educator's call to educate, and how does that affect learners?** Our values and beliefs provide a foundation for our thinking and the decisions that shape the culture of the classroom community.

- **How is teaching a voyage of self- and collaborative discovery?** This question helps us frame teaching diverse learners as a creative act requiring curiosity and a willingness to improvise and adjust so that we can meet their needs and help them build their skills.
- **How does educator empowerment contribute to student empowerment?** The steps educators take to model the actions and attitudes of empowerment help students internalize these behaviors and mindsets and become empowered themselves.
- **How can educators model empowerment?** Conscious deployment of a positive mindset can help individuals overcome barriers and navigate obstacles. Demonstrating this in various ways for our students affirms the importance of agency and choice.

The Call to Educate

To foster empowerment in our students, it helps to understand the factors underlying the call to be an educator. While each of us has our own reasons for entering the teaching profession, and still different ones for staying in it, a common key motivator for doing this work is what behavioral sciences writer Daniel Pink (2009) calls *drive*—the intrinsic motivation to seek autonomy, mastery, and purpose. Here is U.S. Supreme Court Justice Ruth Bader Ginsburg alluding to the source of her own drive while speaking about the importance of having a sense of purpose:

> If you want to be a true professional, you will do something outside yourself, something to repair tears in your community. Something to make life a little better for people less fortunate than you. That's what I think a meaningful life is—living not for oneself, but for one's community. (Sullivan, 2017, para. 3)

Motivation, in general, is often grounded in the ability to exercise choice. Think of how a young person who spent her teenage years resisting her parents' demands that she clean up her room or clear the dinner table might, when she gets her first apartment, take pride in keeping it spotless. Now cleaning up is a personal choice rather than an obligation imposed by a disapproving authority figure.

The more we, as teachers, can connect to our own motivation—including what calls us to be educators—the better our ability to model empowerment and foster it in students. Take a look at Sheila Reid's thoughts on what motivates and shapes her practice.

Take a Closer Look: A Personal Call to Educate

I have been a teacher for over 40 years. In college, I resisted education as a career option and intentionally attended a school that offered no teacher preparatory courses. But, after observing in a Montessori school post-graduation, then volunteering as an assistant there, I became completely captivated by the transformative power of teaching.

The transformation works in two directions: by supporting the unfolding development of the student and by working the same powerful magic on me, as the teacher. The prospect of igniting the imagination of a child through a well-delivered lesson or designing a corner of the learning environment that begs to be explored inspires me to dig deeper into a subject, observe a student's response more closely, and challenge my powers of creativity, patience, and perseverance. My students and I are collaborators; I may have years and experience on my side, but they have unfettered imaginations and uninhibited reasoning on theirs. How many times have I been grateful to wait out a roundabout solution to a math problem or a literary argument that finally resolves into refreshingly original conclusion? When I can maintain the humility of a novice and regard my young learners as partners in the learning process, the rewards to us both are profound.

—Sheila Reid, reading and writing specialist, Chemung Valley Montessori School, Elmira, New York

In his book *Drive,* Pink (2009) explains that workplace motivation can be analyzed by examining three elements: autonomy, mastery, and purpose. Let's try applying that approach.

Autonomy

Autonomy is when we feel that we have a voice in making, or at least influencing, the decisions that affect our lives. It results from having our opinions, decisions, and actions receive the support (or at least the respect) of those around us, including our supervisors, colleagues, and others. Our sense of autonomy increases as our unique and innate interests, strengths, and talents are acknowledged and valued, and when we are recognized for our competence and skill.

Teachers' sense of autonomy faces an external threat in that the practice of teaching is not always seen by outsiders as what it is: a complex, research-informed, art-and-science-based profession. Teaching is not the application of formulaic practices. It requires us to integrate our emotional responses, intuitions, personal experiences, and enthusiasms to connect to other people. At its most meaningful and satisfying, our profession invites us and inspires us. It asks us to observe, reflect, and then devise plans that we believe will work in a particular situation and with specific students. And it also asks us to notice the unique responses, actions, and interests of our students and to reflect, create, and test plans that will enhance their understanding and capabilities.

In the classroom, teachers need autonomy to make continuous, responsive adjustments to our students. Doing our job well means adjusting from moment to moment, hour to hour, day to day, week to week, and year to year. In addition, as our student population shifts and changes, so must our methods for connecting with them. Let's say you are a 4th grade teacher working in a low-income rural area in the northeastern United States. Just before the school year begins, you review your student roster. You have a class of 26 students, and six have identified learning disabilities—two students who are deaf, one with a diagnosis of autism, and three with an auditory processing disability. In addition, the class includes five English learners—three Spanish speakers from Puerto Rico who experienced the trauma of Hurricane Maria and two students who are recent immigrants from Vietnam and speak Vietnamese. How would you go about establishing positive, academically and emotionally supportive connections within a classroom that has this broad array of differences?

Decisions on how to proceed in such circumstances—increasingly common in classrooms throughout the United States—should be driven by the interests, enthusiasms, emotional needs, cultural values, and home communication styles of the students in the classrooms. Often, this means employing different strategies simultaneously; it's the only way teachers can possibly meet such a diverse range of needs. For example, a strategy that might work with the general population of students, or with students who love expressing themselves, or with students who are excited about math might not be successful with students who have sensory processing disorders, who are beginning learners of English, who are shy, or who consider themselves bad at math. Teachers need to plan for the various contingencies and have responses in their pocket, whether that be another strategy or collaborative support from a co-teacher or specialist. It's essential that we build in flexibility, and to do that, we need flexibility ourselves.

Teachers' capacity to be effective on our own and in partnership with others depends on an ability to exercise autonomous decision making and apply insights, inspirations, intuitions, and creative solutions. We need the latitude to exercise professional judgment and depart from standardized methods of instruction determined by administration or an overriding imperative (often self-imposed) to "teach to the test." Every educator needs to be free to provide students with memorable experiences or personal connections to learning concepts without having to endure a critical evaluation or a reprimand for not being on page 84 of the math text at 10:30 a.m. during an administrator's walkthrough.

At the same time, the privilege of professional autonomy calls for our willingness to responsibly surrender what we personally enjoy or see as best in order to more effectively support those who share responsibility for our students and the commitment to serving them as best we can. Practicing this kind of collaborative interdependence means taking into account multiple perspectives at once, including the needs and rules of the institutions in which we work and the needs or desires of our students' families and our colleagues and supervisors. We must also be willing to take guidance from our administrative supervisors while collaborating productively with other professionals, attending to diversity, being socially responsible, and, of course, adapting to our students' ever-changing needs, interests, and motivations.

Ultimately, our work as educators asks us to continually reflect on our practice in order to identify, acknowledge, and value our strength of purpose and our skills. An example is Jennifer Hunter, an instructional coach in Massachusetts. She refers to the strengths that she brings to the work, and she underscores the importance of being vulnerable and honest with herself rather than always in control.

Take a Closer Look: Autonomy Through Self-Reflection

As an instructional language coach, my primary role is to support the teachers who work in language-based classrooms and their English-learning students. Most of what I do is work collaboratively with other educators.

I think that through teaching, you learn very quickly what your strengths and weaknesses are. There is nothing like planning or teaching a lesson to tell you what you do well and what you need to work on. Being self-reflective is really powerful during this time. As educators, we really have to be honest with ourselves and others if we want to grow in a specific area. I find that when a teacher opens up to me as their coach, they are coming to me in a vulnerable position and asking for help. When I work with a teacher, I also find that I learn about my own strengths and weaknesses. For instance, I have a lot of experience in the content areas of reading and writing and prefer to coach in those areas. I find that I tend to feel more apprehensive when working in the content area of math, especially in the upper elementary grades. Therefore, I ask a lot more questions and do a lot more listening to get as much information as I can when I coach a teacher in math. I try to be honest with them and explain that I am learning, too.

—Jennifer Hunter, instructional coach, Brockton, Massachusetts

Mastery

Responsible educators are always striving to strengthen their practice and hone the skills necessary to help all students succeed. This quest for mastery is generally motivated by the desire to be our best selves professionally and, according to Pink (2009), by the satisfaction of receiving accurate and precise feedback on our efforts to strengthen our practice. Let's say, for example, that you attend a professional development session where you encounter new ideas for working more successfully with students on the autism spectrum. What goes on in your mind as you successfully implement what you've learned?

In our experience, new ideas for practice trigger teachers to reflect on what might enhance or extend what is working in current practice and address what is not. We experiment with these ideas, take note of their effects, and gain satisfaction in a job better done and students better served. For teachers, satisfaction of pursuing mastery is intellectual *and* practical, personal *and* altruistic.

Purpose

Teaching is challenging work, but most of us who identify as educators would say it's worth the effort. There is great meaning in contributing to the lives of others *and* in being part of an interdependent professional community working for a common purpose. Indeed, the excitement that we feel in working with our students and their families, and in teaming with our colleagues and others, is motivating in and of itself.

Michael describes it as being "driven to teach" (Silverstone, 2017). He taught older students initially, but the early developmental experiences of his son and memories of his own childhood learning eventually drew him to teach younger ones. Being an elementary teacher has brought more satisfaction and meaning to Michael's life. He especially values being able to use his adult perspective and the empathy that he's gained over time to meet the needs of his students and their families.

Pink (2009) describes the type of motivation that Michael has experienced as the quest to work for something that is larger and more important than ourselves. This purpose drives educators to maintain productivity and engagement, because we see how doing the work helps us realize our personal goals and mission.

Teaching as a Voyage of Self- and Collaborative Discovery

Self-exploration and growth toward mastery can be a voyage of discovery. It involves continuous efforts to work successfully with students who have different interests and temperaments, different histories of school success and struggle, and different levels of academic language and literacy. They may be coping with poverty, homelessness, trauma, violence, or chronic stress. They may be living in two-parent homes, single-parent or grandparent-led homes, foster homes, shelters, institutions (such as for incarcerated youth), or residential schools. They may be trying to meet the expectations of demanding or stressed parents or guardians.

Such a diversity of student backgrounds requires that we take time to adapt our methods and curricula. We also need to be practiced in infusing new life and approaches into well-used materials. No matter where we work or what we do, the challenge of continually strengthening our work with various and ever-changing student and family populations, curriculum, and classroom conditions should be a powerful motivator.

Consider the example of a teacher working in a district that decides to replace its current mathematics curriculum. The introduction of new materials and methods puts the teacher in the same position as the learners, and his or her attitude about using the new curriculum requires the same model of learning that we expect from our students—being curious and willing to explore, and being able to roll with the inevitable mistakes that are part of the journey of discovery. Teachers who enjoy the journey are the ones who take pleasure in the challenge and its rewards. No real challenge is ever easy, but there are steps you can take to fortify yourself.

Self-Care

Earlier, we cited Justice Ruth Bader Ginsburg's belief in service as a driver for professionalism. What is also true about Justice Ginsburg's commitment to professionalism is that it includes a strong element of self-care. Part of her regular regimen includes strenuous workouts that would be challenging for anyone, let alone a person in her 80s (Miller, 2017). While we might be enamored of Justice Ginsburg's grit, it is practical to approach any demanding profession, including teaching, with a strong physical, emotional, and even spiritual foundation. For this reason, many of educators find that activities such as exercise, meditation, and yoga broaden their awareness and renew their energy and spirit for the essential work they do.

Working from Individual and Collective Strengths

Motivational psychologist Abraham Maslow (1987) coined the term *positive psychology* to describe human behavior that is directed toward fulfillment. More recent research has expanded our understanding of the term, which is now used to describe the natural assets, capacities, and qualities that inspire people to pursue self-improvement. One of the most powerful of these is positive feedback. We are all individually and collectively motivated by both the encouragement we *receive from* others and the encouragement we *give to* others. As such, positive psychology looks beyond the individual self to the positive possibilities of working and partnering together. According to Lewis (2016), we can find new ideas for connection by tapping into our collective ideas and strengths and the strengths of the organizations in which we work.

How Teacher Motivation Affects Learners

Research has demonstrated the effectiveness of instructional arrangements in which students learn from one another, and in many classrooms, collaborative activities have supplanted traditional lecture-based approaches. Indeed, the ever-changing environment in which we teach underlines the importance of collaboration as a pragmatic practice as well as a professional norm.

Being Collaborative

Once upon a time, it was common for teachers to close the classroom door and just do their own thing with little outside influence or oversight. In recent years, there has been a concerted effort to improve the quality of education by focusing on evaluating and "improving" individual educators. That emphasis on individual responsibility for developing and maintaining (and demonstrating and documenting) skills, and the fact that students' performance on standardized tests has been used to reflect the relative "value" of a teacher in comparison to colleagues, have helped create a culture in which teachers may feel it's dangerous to discuss areas of challenge, to ask for and get help, or to work collaboratively toward making improvements. Yet exactly these sorts of open, collegial discussions about what is challenging are what makes growth possible. Sharing our hopes and even our struggles and concerns, without fear of stigma or reprisal, is essential to succeeding in the ongoing work of refining and improving teaching.

We have to be comfortable with being works in progress—with being open and flexible, and asking questions that lead to new and different solutions and ideas. We have to be willing to try new approaches, collaborate with others, and listen without judgment to different perspectives. That may sound idealistic, but there are practical reasons for doing so:

1. It allows us to share tasks and, in doing so, lessens the amount of work that we would otherwise need to do on our own.

2. It enables us to learn from each other.

3. It helps us increase our effectiveness as educators.

4. It sends a message to students that school is a place where support and the collective wisdom of others is available. This message invites a willingness to contribute and to risk learning new things, knowing that a classroom can be a place where responsibilities as well as talents and energy can be shared for the success of all.

Being Diversity Attuned

Paying attention to the diverse students and families with whom we work involves much more than knowing that students are members of certain racial, cultural, or linguistic groups (e.g., African American, Asian, white, deaf, Spanish-speaking). While this information is important to know, it can lack nuance. If our goal is to honor students and their families so that they feel safe, a sense of belonging, valued, and competent, the term *diversity attuned* is much more richly layered and complex than generic categories such as these.

Developmental psychologist Mary Gauvain (2001) explains the importance of understanding child development as being shaped by a child's observations, exposure, and interactions with parents or guardians, family members, their community, and beyond. It includes such routines and repeated exposures as observing how parents or guardians interact with each other and with others at home and elsewhere. As such, children's sense of identity reflects the places where they develop an understanding the world in which they live (Gauvain, 2001, 2013; Zacarian, Alvarez-Ortiz, & Haynes, 2017). Figure 2.1 illustrates the types of influence that shape a child's identity.

Being diversity attuned means taking steps beyond categorizing students into groups and then making decisions based on perceived stereotypes. It involves taking time to get to know all students and their personal, social, cultural, and world experiences so that we can build relationships and instructional programs based on these understandings.

For example, let's say you are a high school teacher in and a high percentage of your students share common demographic characteristics with students who are statistically more likely to underachieve or drop out of school. Here are some

FIGURE 2.1

Interactive Influences Shaping a Child's Identity

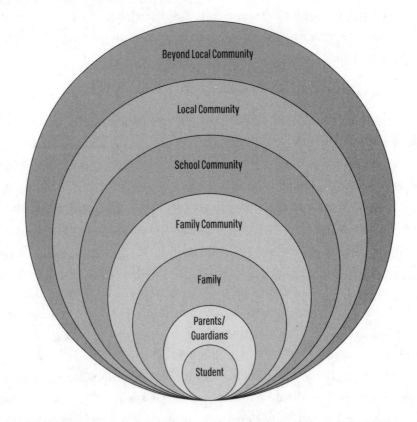

Source: Adapted from *Teaching to Strengths: Supporting Students Living with Trauma, Violence, and Chronic Stress* (p. 139) by D. Zacarian, L. Alvarez-Ortiz, and J. Haynes, 2017, Alexandria, VA: ASCD. Copyright 2017 by ASCD.

important questions to ask yourself as you start to think about being diversity attuned:

- What is (or was) my reaction to having these students in my class? Do I find myself feeling disempowered and less hopeful? What do I base that feeling on?
- Do I think about the obstacles I face in teaching these students, or do I focus on what we might achieve together and the power I have to support their empowerment and success?

- Have I thought about what I can do to boost my own confidence in my ability to teach historically underserved students and ensure that they are successful?

Being Socially Responsible

The type of agency that we want students to use in order to have a voice about the world around them is something we, as teachers, also must possess. However, teaching is rarely thought of as a political act. "I don't have a political bone in my body," a colleague once told us. Yet she was also someone who championed a literacy workshop model for our school district, joined a study group to learn how to improve students' social-emotional learning, applied for an opening as an interim assistant principal, and served as a delegate to the annual meeting of our statewide teachers union. Each of these actions reflected her agency as a responsible educator.

In an era when much of the public political discourse is incendiary and uncompromising, maintaining distance from the fray of politics is an urge that many of us instinctively understand. But politics doesn't just mean electoral campaigning or being a member of a political party. It also includes influencing one another through our values and participation in shared public life. As educators and as public servants, there are practical and moral constraints on our expressions of political opinion during the workday (and sometimes beyond) so that we do not, even by implication, use our authority in the classroom to privilege our personal views over those of our students. But, like absolute objectivity in journalism, political neutrality by educators is an impossibility. We influence others politically, whether we are aware of it or not, by discovering what is consistently important to us and living it. Our practice is guided by countless choices between seeming opposites. Consider the following:

- It is important to establish warm and empathetic connections with students; it is also important to be firm and somewhat neutral so that students can feel their own independence.
- A quiet classroom allows better concentration; an active classroom filled with energetic conversation fosters communication and collaboration.
- An effective educator works at home on the weekends to plan lessons, formulate feedback, and better serve students; an effective educator spends

nonwork time as an activist on behalf of public policies to support public education and to advocate for the health care, nutrition, and overall well-being of children and families.

In these pairs of opposing actions, there are no right answers. Though they contradict each other, all are simultaneously true and valid.

Teaching for a full school year is often compared to participating in a marathon. To summon the immense amount of energy required to be intellectually, physically, and emotionally prepared to serve the demands of the role, educators need to rest sometimes in the confidence that the choices they make are coming from their core values and are consistent with their mission as human beings who have chosen teaching as a profession. Connecting the choices that we make to our deeply held values helps us sustain our efforts and draw energy from that work.

 Time for Reflection

1. Make a list of the values and beliefs that motivate you as an educator, using this sentence starter: "What I believe, what motivates me, and what gets me up in the morning and keeps me going even when it's difficult is. . . ."
2. Make a second list of the things about you—your personal characteristics—that your students, their families, and your colleagues count on you to exhibit.
3. In what ways have your teaching practices demonstrated the first list's values and beliefs and the second list's personal characteristics?

Other Ways to Model Empowerment

The year 2018 was notable for the number of teacher protests throughout the United States. In West Virginia, Oklahoma, Arizona, Colorado, and North Carolina, teachers also went on strike. A CNN article called it "the school year teachers reached their breaking point" (Yan, 2018, para. 1). These collective actions were motivated by reduced public spending on education, stagnant wages, changes to pensions and benefits, and a generalized belief that the profession had become economically impossible.

Teachers were not alone in their protests. Students also led walkouts and protests to advocate for legislative restrictions on firearms sales in response to many episodes of gun violence in schools. In addition, in the fall of 2017, students in Denver, Los Angeles, Tucson, and many other cities walked out of classes to protest the federal government's decision to rescind the immigration status of 800,000 young people who were in the process of becoming U.S. citizens under the Deferred Action for Childhood Arrivals naturalization program.

The waves of organized protests and actions by students and teachers highlight empowerment's important role in effecting change. It fuels action to identify problems that demand a response and inspires us to raise our voices on behalf of the larger community of teachers and learners in hopes of influencing public policy. We can increase both our capacity to act as empowered educators and our capacity to empower students by developing our own ability to adapt and be resilient.

Being Adaptive

Technology has brought tremendous change. It has made previously unimaginable forms of communication possible, and it continues to evolve in ways that have made enterprises such as Khan Academy, MOOCs (massive open online courses), YouTube, and social networking part of our everyday vernacular. In the classroom, technology has expanded teachers' instructional toolbox and made it possible for many students not to just access more content more efficiently but also to efficiently create content of their own. At the same time, technological advances have led to a deeper divide between educators, students, and families with access to technology and those with outdated computers, limited or interrupted online access, or a lack of financial means to afford technology's latest advances.

Being adaptive involves much more than possessing technological savvy or making education work without it. It also requires that teachers be adaptive in a range of ways in our everyday practice. With student absences due to illnesses, new students arriving during the school year, changing curriculum, limited (or no) finances, large class sizes, and more, teachers have become increasingly adaptive to changing times and circumstances, both expected and unexpected. Our empowerment relies on us being able to roll with the punches in our ever-changing workplace.

The adaptations we make on a regular basis include responding to challenging situations in ways that exemplify the type of positive relationships we value most in our students and colleagues (rather than reacting by being critical) and taking time to listen for and amplify the strengths and goodness that we see in others.

Take, for example, Jessie, a middle school student who, more often than not, arrived late to her math class and spent the period slumped in her seat. In an effort to be adaptive, Jessie's teacher sought ways to help her get to class on time and pique her interest in participating. Now, every time Jessie is seated before the bell, her teacher tells her how genuinely happy she is to see her. The shift this teacher has made—from seeing Jessie negatively (the kid who is always late and doesn't care) to seeing her in a positive light (a fount of potential)—speaks to the teacher's capacity to adapt to the challenges of the profession. Jessie's teacher has embraced her own power, and that is making a difference.

Being Resilient

The pressures teachers face are more than you can count on two hands. To name just a few, there is the stubborn pressure to elevate test scores, of course, but there's also the stress of having to make do with limited funding, handle increased class sizes, navigate outdated materials, and work in crumbling physical environments. Another important pressure today's educators face, regardless of where we work, is staving off a secondary posttraumatic stress response associated with teaching so many students living with trauma, violence, and chronic stress of their own (Zacarian et al., 2017). All of these pressures highlight the importance of being resilient. Our capacity to be empowered is strengthened by acknowledging the stressors that we experience and by celebrating and developing our capacity to deal with them.

Some Practical Strategies

Taking care of ourselves so we can better take care of others requires consciously seeking and providing ourselves with supports that sustain energy, equanimity, and a sense of agency as educators and as human beings. It's akin to the preflight safety instructions aimed at parents and caregivers: "Please secure your mask before assisting others." We have gathered together here a few physical and emotional self-care strategies, some more obvious than others, that can make a crucial difference in your day-to-day ability to model empowerment.

Strategies for Physical Self-Care

- **Stay hydrated.** It's easy to overlook how easily we can become dehydrated, which depletes our mental clarity, stamina, and ability to ward off illness. It might not be obvious when we aren't drinking enough water. A helpful strategy is to keep a water bottle on hand and to drink from it regularly: when you wake up, during work, at meals, and before sleep. These habits can go a long way in supporting our health (U.S. National Library of Medicine, 2019).

- **Get daytime light exposure.** Working in classrooms with limited natural light or during the seasons with reduced daylight hours can have a deleterious effect on health, mood, and sleep. Indoor light boxes used in your home or classroom can mitigate these effects (Court, 2010).

- **Pay attention to nutrition.** One way to maintain health and wellness is by choosing foods that avoid excess sugar, salt, artificial colorings and flavorings, preservatives, and trans fats and that leave you feeling healthier (Wolfram, 2019).

- **Exercise.** Regular moderate exercise helps maintain our strength and endurance. But it also can help prevent or manage a host of health conditions, such as high blood pressure, Type 2 diabetes, depression, and anxiety. It also promotes quality sleep. Make sure to schedule exercise during times that are convenient and enjoyable so that it becomes a sustainable habit (Mayo Clinic, 2019).

- **Don't skimp on sleep.** Medical research shows that having at least seven hours of sleep a night promotes health, improves alertness, and allows the body to repair itself and prevent chronic health issues such as cardiovascular disease, diabetes, and obesity. Studies have measured the effect of being awake for more than 18 hours as equivalent to having a blood alcohol content of 0.05 percent (Centers for Disease Control and Prevention, 2018). Be intentional about creating the conditions conducive to good sleep, setting screen-use curfews, and making the protection of sleep time a priority.

- **Get proper health care.** All of us need to follow a health care regimen (e.g., regular medical and dental care) for our own well-being and to prevent illness.

Strategies for Emotional Self-Care

- **Make time for quiet and reflection.** Routine practices that focus your attention on something external to yourself and enable you to reach a relaxed state are important. These practices can include mindfulness exercises, meditation, yoga, martial arts, journal writing, reading, cooking, painting, and spending time with a pet.
- **Offer and receive support.** We all need people who see us in a caring light. A school community can provide you with opportunities to support others and celebrate successes. Making time to create these kinds of caring connections can provide you with more energy, rather than taking it away. At the same time, you may wish to seek guidance from outside supports such as spiritual, clinical, and therapeutic counselors. This can be especially helpful when you are feeling overwhelmed. Having a person who can help you process these feelings and put them into a perspective that lets you move forward can be invaluable.
- **Spread positive energy.** Just as you might help clean and care for common work areas, you might also want to consider ways you could contribute to an energy-giving, care-filled environment at your school, even if it means cultivating a variety of oases in a place filled with challenges. Here are some ways to do this:
  - *Contribute to a sense of community.* This includes greeting people by name, smiling, holding doors open, and other small gestures that demonstrate care.
  - *Build relationships with your students' families.* This can be done by going out of your way to share good news about their child, even when things are not going well. Indeed, highlighting anything, large or small, contributes to the sense that parents and guardians are educators' allies and creates positive energy for facing challenges.

– *Aim for a 3:1 (or higher) ratio of positive to negative comments.* A range of studies of teachers and students (as well as of employers and employees and married couples) find that a ratio of three to five positive interactions to one negative interaction leads to better relationships and greater success and satisfaction. Research also shows that people react far more strongly to a negative or critical comment than a positive one and that it takes many more positive interactions to balance out the negative. In addition, it is important to consciously deliver negative or corrective responses in ways that engage a person positively as opposed to shaming or embarrassing them. Knowledge of this ratio can be very helpful for framing our own experiences; seeing reasons for gratitude can empower us to feel encouraged, capable, and positive about challenges (Pozen, 2013).

High school teacher Christine Sand describes the steps she takes to stay resilient and be a "work in progress." She tells us that rather than avoid hard conversations for fear that they might lead to her feeling too frustrated, she now faces challenges head-on, because she's found doing so helps her feel happier and more empowered.

Take a Closer Look: Resilience

For a long time, I thought I would eventually get used to the circumstances of teaching if I just plugged away, but that's not the case. Resilience is an active and conscious pursuit. When I feel worn down by the demands of teaching high-needs students, or when difficulties begin to percolate due to strained relationships between students, other teachers, or the administration, I find it's better not to suppress my emotions; if I do that, they just continue to build.

If I don't allow myself to feel what I'm feeling, it becomes hard to focus on tasks. Even meaningful assignments that cultivated learning that students (and I) had worked hard on become "another thing."

So what do I do? I write it out. I have a notebook, and I make a T-chart that has the problem on one side and my solutions on the other. Before I write each solution, though, I envision what it will look like in my setting. For example, if students are using cell phones in the classroom,

I tend to be personally offended that they are not taking the work seriously or are taking the time we have for granted. I let the episode play out and think about each solution. It looks like an "if/then" scenario: *If* I bring a box for students to put a phone in that they're using, *then* what will that look like? Most likely, it will be refusal, denial, and embarrassment for the students. So that solution doesn't make the list. I continue this process until I generate a list that is less about my control and more about the culture and community that I'm hoping to instill in the classroom, solutions like one-on-one conversations or asking students to write a dialogue to show what *they* think my approach should be. I think this fosters empathy. I need for us to relate to each other and for me not be "the controller." It's emotionally taxing to try to control not just possessions but bathroom access, sidebar conversations, cursing, and on and on.

When I cultivate my own resilience, I feel relieved, empowered, and happier. I find I'm able to be more involved and less disconnected from the culture of my classroom.

—Christine Sand, high school teacher, Boston Public Schools, Boston, Massachusetts

 Time for Reflection

Drawing from Christine's discussion, describe the steps and actions that you have taken to acknowledge your strengths and capacity to be a resilient and empowered educator as well as a "work in progress" who is building resilience.

* * * * *

In the next chapter, we continue examining empowerment by looking more closely at how educators can construct the physical environment to communicate that *all* students are welcome, valued, acknowledged, and encouraged to be contributing members of the school community.

Creating a Physical Environment That Supports Empowerment

The physical environment of a classroom has the power to positively or negatively affect students' learning, engagement, social-emotional development, sense of belonging—and yes, their feeling of empowerment. This is true whether you teach in a self-contained or open space that can accommodate 30 or more students, a small space for a handful of students, or a multipurpose room used for a variety of functions and occasions. While educators might not have much choice about which rooms we will teach in (more often than not, they are assigned to us), there are still many decisions we can make to create an environment that truly supports student empowerment.

Architect William Bradley warns educators that "if we design something reluctantly, halfway, or after the fact, students may get the impression that that for which we design is unimportant. Even as we attempt to teach them to incorporate, celebrate, or be sensitive to certain ideas and concepts, we may be contradicting ourselves in design" (Rivero, 2004, para. 2). This chapter focuses on how we can set up or modify our student's physical learning environment to align with our values and support student dialogue and contributions. Here are the topics we will explore and the reasons why:

- **Crafting an inclusive design.** How a classroom is set up has the power to convey the essential message that *all* students are welcome, valued, and acknowledged as active members of an inclusive classroom community.

- **Understanding classroom design as a balancing act.** Many schools and classrooms were built years before collaboration, respecting and accommodating diverse populations, and technology became essential functions in education. This reality challenges us to change what we can and get the most out of what we can't.

- **Designing to support collaboration.** It's so important that classroom design (or redesign) be driven by a belief in the value of learning together and a commitment to removing barriers to equal participation among diverse learners.

- **Promoting agency and initiative.** Involving students in decisions about the design and norms of the classroom environment is a way to help them navigate that environment more independently and be empowered as learners.

- **Promoting respect for diversity.** To feel like members of their learning community, and to make sure all members are valued, students need to see aspects of their cultural, ethnic, and racial identity reflected back to them.

- **Creating a learning studio targeted for mutual empowerment.** Every classroom must accommodate its community of learners; embracing flexibility as the guiding principle of classroom configuration is the way to pursue this objective.

- **Infusing an empowered use of technology.** We can't afford to overlook the degree to which technology can enhance students' social-emotional and academic learning communication.

Let's dig in.

Crafting an Inclusive Design

Our various teaching spaces and the students we serve vary so widely that it is impossible to create a one-size-fits-all, gold standard design for an empowered classroom. However, there are key design choices that can help students feel that the classroom is their space—and a place where they belong and have a voice.

Our most useful guidance for evaluating and adapting your specific space to empower your specific students is to ask what design features will best support everyone's ability to learn and be collaborative. Ask yourself this question, and ask your students too. You want to co-create with them a physical environment over which they feel a sense of ownership and in which they feel comfortable and confident. As a reflection of student ownership, the classroom environment ought to change throughout the school year in concert with students' evolving needs and interests. Think of how the furniture in a child's room might transition from a crib to a bed, and how the décor might change from trains to dinosaurs to pop stars to symbolically reflect the child's growing sense of individuality.

As educators, our priorities and values are implicit in our classrooms' design. The actions teachers take in designing classrooms are akin to creating an ecosystem that "enfolds several dimensions such as social, cultural, architectural, and technological" to work together in harmony (Sardinha, Almeida, & Barbas, 2017, p. 39). In other words, the classroom design represents much more than a space where students are seated to learn language arts, mathematics, science, and so forth. Rather, the design itself embodies the central idea that learning happens when those who comprise a classroom community (its students, teacher, and others) socialize, interact, and work together (e.g., individually, in pairs, in small groups) to form an interconnected, inclusive, and even interdependent collaborative ecosystem. Further, this happens most readily when the design is orchestrated to support everyone's successful membership.

We remember visiting a classroom whose community included a teaching assistant assigned to work with a student who is blind. One design feature we noted was that the assistant's and teacher's desks, located at the back of the classroom, were the same size and sat side by side. The teacher explained to us that this intentional design was a way to convey a message to students that the assistant is an equal of the teacher, and everyone in the classroom is an equal member of the learning community. Another example is a classroom community that includes a student who uses a wheelchair. Rather than have the student sit in a designated area (like movie theaters often do), everyone in the class works together to ensure that their classmate is included in each paired, small-group, and whole-class activity. As their classroom shifts from one grouping pattern to another, the whole class makes sure that there is enough aisle space for their classmate to move about the room in his wheelchair. These two classroom design choices communicate the value *we are all equal members of an inclusive community*. Everyone works in concert with one another to support their individual and collective success.

 Time for Reflection

1. How do the inclusive design examples provided reflect a belief in empowerment and encourage empowerment?
2. Describe an additional example of classroom features that promote inclusiveness and ensure that all students are seen, valued, and acknowledged as competent members of their classroom community.

Understanding Classroom Design as Balancing Act

Some of the messages a classroom sends are a function of the architectural decisions that were made when the building was constructed. Reality requires that we work with what we have, but conscience demands that we get as close as we can to a design that communicates our empowerment objectives and values.

First, the context. In 1874, the first big boom of public-school construction in the United States was kicked off by the Kalamazoo decision, a Michigan Supreme Court ruling that ordered that public schools be funded by local property taxes. Many new school buildings were built in the wake of this decision, increasing numbers of students filled them, and for the next 50 years or so, the priorities in school construction were efficiency, standardization, and maximization of space (Baker, 2012). Population increases and the nation's application of industrial manufacturing efficiency produced a factory model of school design in which desks were packed into rows and classrooms into multistory buildings (Baker, 2012). In later eras, including the postwar school construction boom from 1945 to 1960 and the architectural experimentation era from 1960 to 1980, the values of the times left lasting imprints on school building design in terms of shape, size, use of natural light, building materials, acoustics, air quality, and open space layouts.

The philosophy and values of any particular era are expressed in the design of public buildings, but the reality is that these buildings survive a long time. A significant number of classrooms in the United States were constructed long before collaboration, respecting and accommodating diverse populations, and technology emerged as important functions in education. Balancing past and current best practices is not a simple task. However, modifications—both personal additions we make to our classrooms as individuals and larger-scale architectural modifications initiated and underwritten by the district—help make learning spaces more functional. The aim is to work within the parameters we have to get as close as we can to a design that promotes the values that we are seeking: collaboration, agency and initiative, awareness of diversity, social responsibility, and adaptability.

Promoting Collaboration

There are a variety of classroom design protocols you might consult when making practical decisions about the kind of desk or table configurations that are conducive to collaboration, providing spacing for conversation and group work, and so on. Certainly draw from these, but it is also essential that any design or redesign action you undertake be driven by the belief that, in schools, *we each matter to each other,* and all of us—teachers, students, and families alike—are in it together, charged with taking responsibility to co-create a community that makes education work for everyone (Zacarian & Silverstone, 2015).

For the purpose of classroom design, this means considering ways to remove obstacles to equal participation in order to account for differences among students pertaining to visual and auditory acuity, mobility, height, sensory stimulation, and more. Our respectful and unconditional commitment to take into account the needs of all members of our learning communities is, by extension, also a commitment to their parents and guardians, families, and family communities.

A small example of this type of thinking is taking time to ask questions such as "How might we change our classroom design to accommodate a blind student and the assistant assigned to work with the student to ensure that each is comfortable, secure, and capable of working confidently as contributing members to the whole community?" Similar questions should be asked about every student, making sure to consider each student's particular characteristics and challenges, including but not limited to differences or disabilities.

 Time for Reflection

1. Describe the physical environment of your classroom (or a classroom you recently worked in) in relation to how it promotes equal participation for all and supports collaboration among all students.
2. How does your classroom design reflect the demographics of your students?

Promoting Agency and Initiative

Making decisions about the physical environment from the perspective of the learner, rather than the adult exercising power (such as the teacher), is a transformational act. When classroom tools are readily available to students, when furniture is fitted to their actual size, and when sinks and cabinets are mounted at levels that allow all students to access them independently, the message is *this is your room; you belong here* (Center for Responsive Schools, 2001, 2015).

To take this one step further, when students have independent access and can see a consistent organization scheme in the design of the classroom, dependence on adults can be replaced with student self-reliance. This idea of a prepared environment increasing student independence is described by William Maier, director of faculty and curriculum development at the Lexington Montessori School near Boston.

Take a Closer Look: How Classroom Preparation Promotes Independence

I think all the ways that we make the environment belong to the kids help foster independence, because I think that the enemy of empowerment is an overreliance on teacher authority.

The more that kids feel they're being told what to do—managed, directed even—the less agency they feel. When you prepare the learning environment physically so kids can take care of their own needs, they don't need to come to someone else to solve their problems.

When you prepare it organizationally so they can manage themselves—when they don't have to get reminded all the time, and they don't have to get nagged and hounded—they feel in charge of the decisions that they make. As a result, they have the sense of being responsible for their own performance and for the results of those performances. And it seems to me that those things are the root of empowerment.

—William Maier, Lexington Montessori School, Lexington, Massachusetts

There are any number of practical ways that teachers can invite students to feel and be more empowered to take action and make choices in the classroom environment—everything from ensuring they are familiar with the purposes and tools of independent learning stations, to soliciting their help for reorganizing and modifying the classroom, to setting up space to display their work and evidence of conceptual understanding.

Time for Reflection

The table on page 48 lists three collaborative design options. Take a minute to think about them, and use check marks to indicate how important each seems to you.

Ask colleagues to engage in this reflection activity and then compare your responses.

Design Option	Very Important	Important	Not Very Important
Devote time at the beginning of the school year or term to orient students to the various learning stations found in the classroom, including their purpose and the tools used within them.			
Devote time at the beginning of and throughout the school year to brainstorming, proposing, and testing proposals for how the classroom might be reorganized or modified.			
Designate spaces for displaying student work and understandings of the concepts being explored.			

We have asked educators to complete this reflection task in a range of professional development settings. Although we expected the responses to vary, we were surprised by just *how much* they varied. Teachers have different perceptions of the value of students having a hand in the design of their learning space and even different perceptions of students' capacity to do so; these perceptions do not seem to be related to the students' age or grade level. However, we have found that once educators begin to explore the value and ideology of a mutually created physical environment, the responses to the list become more uniform toward a rating of *very important*.

Here are some useful diagnostic questions we ask participants about their classrooms; we'd like you to think about them now.

1. *How can the design that a teacher creates or co-creates with students encourage or discourage each student's learning efforts?* In one of our professional development sessions, a kindergarten teacher at first crossed her arms in front of her chest, signaling her refusal to consider asking young children to participate in such decisions. As she began to explore the notion of co-creating an environment with them, she realized that of course her students had opinions on the placement of tables, chairs, desks, displays, learning stations, and open spaces and were quite willing and able to voice what worked for them! It led this

particular teacher to move the round carpet from the center to the side of the room, where students said it "feels cozier" to sit and work with partners.

2. *How do classroom displays draw students' attention to what is essential to learn?* Many teachers have shared with us how important it is to create visual displays of academic concepts (e.g., on the walls, on tablemats, as handouts). One teacher created a visual display of the key ideas about the colonial period in U.S. history. She co-created a chart with her students labeled "Reasons People Came to the Colonies." Using three sentence strips, small groups of students came to agreement about the three key reasons and taped these onto the chart.

3. *How much involvement and creative decision-making authority do students have in what is displayed on the walls and elsewhere?* Students need to be able to give feedback about how well classroom displays are working. This is essential to ensure that messages and information we present on the wall and elsewhere are successfully received by those for whom they are intended—our students. For example, one high school teacher we worked with displayed a poster of his state's U.S. history standards in a prominent area of his classroom. When he asked students about how it helped them learn, most commented negatively about it and stated that it was written for teachers, not for them (which it was!).

4. *How easy is it for all students to see these displays from their sight lines?* Many teachers have shared with us that student feedback helps them rethink what they display and how much they display.

5. *How do the décor and the images displayed on the walls and elsewhere reflect the cultural, linguistic, gender, racial, and other diversities found among the members of the classroom community?* It's important to reflect your classroom's student diversity in its décor, and we'll delve deeper into why shortly. Right now, we'll just share a quick anecdote about a Massachusetts town that had experienced an influx of South Asian refugees several years back. To ensure that they saw themselves as valued members of the school—to communicate that *they belonged here*—the high school asked students and their families to create a mural depicting their culture. Years later, the mural continues to grace one of the high school's main hallways.

6. *Does the classroom have an appropriate degree of sensory stimulation to encourage calm, concentration, learning, and a sense of well-being?* Getting the balance here is a delicate matter: not too much or too little, but just enough. In their primary grade, multi-age classroom setting, Michael and his colleagues considered the physical adjustments that could be made to maintain calm and productivity while his partner was out on maternity leave. These included rotating the rectangular meeting rug so that the wide-open space of the classroom was reduced and placing worktables for student collaboration in the reclaimed space. They also devoted some wall space to a chart paper sheet on which students tallied assignments to demonstrate their care, focus, and thoroughness. These tallies were graphed onto a class chart that showed the fluctuation and growth of their productive efforts.

 Time for Reflection

Use the following scale to rate your perception of a classroom where you currently work as a teacher, coach, supervisor, or preservice educator (you may also wish to do this with colleagues and discuss your ratings). Consider the actions that you might take to ensure that each of your responses are consistently rating a 5.

1. The physical design of the classroom facilitates learning.

Agree Strongly	Agree	Not Sure	Disagree	Disagree Strongly
5	4	3	2	1

2. The classroom can be used flexibly by small groups, partners, and individuals.

Agree Strongly	Agree	Not Sure	Disagree	Disagree Strongly
5	4	3	2	1

3. The classroom has an appropriate degree of sensory stimulation to encourage calm, concentration, learning, and a sense of well-being.

Agree Strongly	Agree	Not Sure	Disagree	Disagree Strongly
5	4	3	2	1

4. Student identity, student work, and/or student interests are reflected in classroom displays.

Agree Strongly	Agree	Not Sure	Disagree	Disagree Strongly
5	4	3	2	1

Promoting Respect for Diversity

Setting up a classroom to reflect the diversity of the students in it sends a powerful and vital message: *you are seen, you are valued, you are respected.* Just as significantly, the absence of these messages is disempowering. It is important for students to feel a sense of inclusion by having aspects of their identity (cultural, ethnic, racial, etc.) reflected back to them. Visual representations are especially important.

One 3rd grade teacher we worked with displayed a wall map in her classroom that showed the countries that each student's family came from, with accompanying student-generated projects about family artifacts or oral histories. Some students wrote stories about their families, others brought in pictures, and others brought in artifacts. These were displayed alongside the wall map.

As another example, a high school math teacher we worked with gave students free rein to illustrate a mathematical concept they were studying, encouraging them to choose a format that aligned with their interests. Some chose to illustrate the concept in a group-generated drawing, others co-created a poem, others co-wrote a narrative, and still others created a sculpture. All the products were displayed together as testimony to the wealth of creativity and perspectives present in the classroom. Finally, we met a high school science teacher who took time to support students in researching the contributions to the field made by people representing their unique cultures and ethnicities. The students provided portraits and descriptions of these scientists, displaying them in a prominent area of the classroom as testament to their value and expertise.

Students can also play an important role in choosing the furniture layout and creating arrangements that allow for interactive as well as independent learning, particularly as it applies to our diverse classroom environments, where a one-size-fits-all approach may not be as successful as allowing students to have a say in the design choices that work best for each of them. Possibilities include tables that allow for small-group collaboration, lap desks or rugs that make floor work possible, cozy spaces for individual work or quiet reflection, a meeting area that can accommodate the whole class for a group presentation or meeting, a standing area where movement is possible, or a combination of these.

Larry Ferlazzo, a high school English teacher, provides an example of the type of design choices that students make to accommodate individual, paired, and small-group learning simultaneously (Zacarian et al., 2017). Looking for ways to make literature come alive, and knowing that many of his students and their families had emigrated from El Salvador, Larry found a newspaper article about gangs in El Salvador and asked the class if they would like to read it. After they said that they would, he asked whether they wanted to read it in groups or alone. Some wanted to read and talk about the article in pairs, others in groups; those students pushed their desks into these configurations. One student who had been affected by gang violence on a very personal level chose to read the story alone; he moved his desk to the corner of the room and sat with his back to the group. All of these combinations reflected Larry's belief that his students would be empowered by being able to choose the learning design that worked best for them. The goal of any action such as this one is for all of us, students and teachers alike, to choose a classroom design that respects the diversity of the classroom community.

Heterogeneous classrooms and schools have students from a wide range of economic, linguistic, and cultural backgrounds, including students who are English learners, are homeless, have disabilities, and live with adverse childhood experiences. Such students can and often do experience acceptance challenges or status issues that need careful consideration. Our classroom design plans should be adapted so that we may be better prepared to meet students' various academic and social-emotional learning needs (Farmer et al., 2016). The absence of culturally responsive attention can exacerbate the challenges that students face. The type of responsiveness that we must consider includes continuously looking for the strengths that all students possess and validating these so that they are aware of the competencies they bring to the classroom and the design of it (Zacarian et al., 2017).

An example of a culturally responsive classroom adaptation comes from a U.S. history teacher we know. For many years, this teacher had assigned a project in which students interviewed older family members who had lived in the United States during World War II. They displayed their interview projects on the classroom walls and invited relatives to attend a presentation on them. Knowing that several of his students' families were unlikely to have had these experiences, he modified the lesson to be more inclusive. He planned for students to take a walking trip to a nearby senior living center, where they would interview members of their local community, many of whom were World War II veterans and some of whom were Japanese internment camp survivors. Working in small groups, students developed questions for their interviews (e.g., *What was it like for returning soldiers to reunite with their family and family community after the war, particularly for those who returned injured? What was it like for the Japanese members of the community to return after they had been forced to leave?*). To prepare, they held mock interviews with classmates and made modifications that they believed would help the actual interviews run more smoothly. After interviewing the residents of the senior center, the class collectively reflected on the interviews. They stated that the experience helped make the unit of study come alive and raised their awareness about the challenges that people faced.

While this example might not seem directly related to classroom design, how the class ultimately decided to display those interview projects is. At the invitation of their teacher, small groups of students generated various ideas for a project display, after which the whole class came together to make a final decision. They chose to create a display that covered an entire wall of the classroom. At the students' eyeline was a timeline of the Japanese internment and World War II more broadly. Charted above and below were the experiences they documented of the returning soldiers and families.

Another empowering option for classroom design is to create a "home away from home" (Zacarian et al., 2017). This involves inviting students to draw from their own interests and ideas and decorate the classroom so that it is a reflection of them. Seeing so many tokens of individuality from so many students side by side in the classroom is a visible reminder of the learning community's shared ownership of the space. It's a good strategy when you have students who don't see the classroom space as particularly belonging to them or who are resistant to learning. Michael had a wonderful experience with this approach:

> I remember a boy who desperately resisted school structure, either avoiding work or acting miserable much of the time, but who found relief in drawing and tracing animals. He once gave me one of the pictures he had made on tracing paper, and I put it in a frame and placed it on top of a bookshelf in a prominent place in the classroom, where other students were able to see and compliment him on it. The fact that he was being recognized for an accomplishment that was on his own terms seemed to give him another way to think about school and opened the possibility for a successful experience in it. (Zacarian et al., 2017, p. 38)

 Time for Reflection

Use the following scale to rate your perception of a classroom where you currently work as a teacher, coach, supervisor, or preservice educator (you may also wish to do this with colleagues and discuss your ratings). Consider the actions that you might take to ensure that each of your responses are consistently rating a 5.

1. The classroom is well adapted to address the perceptual needs and the cultural, communication, and learning styles of all students.

Agree Strongly	Agree	Not Sure	Disagree	Disagree Strongly
5	4	3	2	1

2. The classroom displays visual evidence of a culture that cares about the collective well-being of the classroom community, school, local community, nation, global community, and/or nature.

Agree Strongly	Agree	Not Sure	Disagree	Disagree Strongly
5	4	3	2	1

Creating a Learning Studio Targeted for Mutual Empowerment

The physical design of our classrooms should accommodate a heterogeneous group of learners *and* include furniture that has the versatility to be used in different ways and can be moved quickly and easily. We describe this flexibility as a *learning studio,* where students are free to experiment together and on behalf of each other to create a classroom design that is empowering for everyone.

An example of this learning studio mindset comes from Robyn Breiman, a Montessori teacher educator and co-director of the Montessori Elementary Teacher Training Collaborative in Lexington, Massachusetts, who told us,

> Children are attracted to organized shelves, I believe, because they are accessible. When things children need to do their work are next to the things that children need to do their next work [assignment], and all parts of the works are available, they become empowered to be more aware of and independent with what they were doing . . . as well as to see the attraction of order, beauty, and access to patterns, which support the development of their mathematical minds.

A second example of the learning studio mindset is provided by an elementary school technology teacher who works in a rural area that doesn't have broadband internet service. There were sometimes electricity brownouts in the old building, causing computers to shut down unexpectedly. When this happened, the teacher wasn't sure what he could do with his technology classes, short of sending students back to their grade-level classrooms. At that time, the furniture in the technology classroom included four rows of tables, each lined with desktop computers facing the front of the classroom. When the brownouts occurred, there didn't seem to be any possibility for anything other than students sitting there facing shut-off computers.

One day, after a lengthy brownout, the teacher decided to spend time brainstorming solutions with each of his classes. He identified the design problem and asked students to collaboratively determine solutions for what to do when the power goes out. Students suggested a range of ideas to reconfigure the design of the classroom, the most popular of which was to go from four rows lined with computers to three, leaving one table without anything on it. That meant that each of his classes would have one row for noncomputer work. Once his students struck on the idea of an empty row, they brainstormed potential solutions for the furniture redesign. Within the week, they collectively voted on a new design. Collectively, each class period devoted time to moving the furniture, computers, and all of the associated wires while testing their hypothesis to see how well all of these changes actually worked. Since that initial brainstorming experience, they have collectively reconfigured the room several times. Each redesign is done in the same fashion and for the same purpose: to make the technology class work when the computers are up and running and when the computers are down. As time has passed, new groups have brainstormed solutions, resulting in a number of creative solutions to what they call the "brownout dilemma."

Our learning studio model, like the technology classroom example, involves a recursive process, illustrated in Figure 3.1.

FIGURE 3.1

The Recursive Process of a Learning Studio

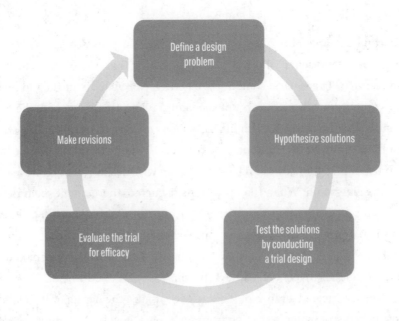

The first stage involves defining the design problem, which might include poor lighting or acoustics, vision barriers (e.g., a wall that juts out into the classroom), a lack of open space for students to move about, a lack of desktop space, and more. Once a design problem has been identified, the second stage is to brainstorm various solutions and collectively select one or more ideas that can be tested. After the ideas have been tested, it's time to evaluate how well the trial worked for everyone, then move on to the next stage: refining the solutions. This learning studio model of experimentation can be very helpful in many ways, but probably the most significant for our discussion is that it underscores students' sense of ownership of the classroom space and empowers them to adjust it for the benefit of all.

 Time for Reflection

Use the following scale to rate your perception of a classroom where you currently work as a teacher, coach, supervisor, or preservice educator (you may also wish to do this with colleagues and discuss your ratings). Consider the actions that you might take to ensure that your response is consistently rating a 5.

1. Students regularly engage in identifying a design problem in their classroom and hypothesizing solutions, testing them, evaluating their efficacy, and making revisions.

Agree Strongly	Agree	Not Sure	Disagree	Disagree Strongly
5	4	3	2	1

Infusing an Empowered Use of Technology

In the mid-1990s, the digital era began with some seemingly modest but useful new tools for communication, and then rapidly exploded to dominate and transform nearly every aspect of our daily lives. It has grown so exponentially that a Nielsen survey found that the average adult spends a whopping 10 hours and 39 minutes per day staring at a TV, tablet, smartphone, video game, or personal computer screen "consuming media" (Howard, 2016). While the effects of this dramatic change are evolving, there is no doubt that technology must be part of our consideration of the physical design of classrooms and schools, as it has the power to enhance students' social-emotional and academic learning communication (Montrieux, Vanderlinde, Schellens, & De Marez, 2015; Yelland, 2006). Helping students be empowered technologically includes safeguarding them from potential harm and supporting their access to and use of technology in classrooms in a way that supports their success in school and in life beyond it.

Some decisions related to technology may appear to be beyond our control. Perhaps it has always been presented to you as something to use, and you have not had the opportunity to critically consider its application in the physical design of the classroom. Whereas 20 years ago, the introduction of technology led to having large clunky desktops sitting in the corner of our classrooms or having computer labs that some of us used a lot and others very little (Montrieux et al., 2015), these days, many schools are fully equipped for technology in classrooms, hallways, and just about everywhere in and outside the school (Minero, 2018). In these schools, connectivity has become so commonplace that educators are working with students in areas that were, just a few years ago, devoted to a different purpose.

An example is the stairwell at Ecole Kenwood French Immersion School. When we say "stairwell," you probably visualize it primarily as a transportation route, where people go up or down steps to get from one level to another. Not at this school. Ecole Kenwood's stairwell is also a space for teaching, socializing, presenting, and collaborating. It's fully wired with projection screens, speakers, and more (Minero, 2018). Perhaps it is the width of the stairwell and the intention that it appears as an amphitheater that makes it so successful. And it shows just how important it is to take time to explore what is possible. In schools across the United States, desktops have given way to laptops, tablets, and SMART Boards, with access to the internet and an overabundance of information just a click away for millions of students and their teachers. We need to consider all these factors when designing our learning spaces.

Here are some tech-related classroom design suggestions to keep in mind:

1. *Examine how you use technology in your classroom to enhance students' social-emotional and academic growth and communication.* For example, students may

not be familiar with the term *horse and buggy* as they read a story, so they might use technology to find an image that explains it. You might make use of translation programs that assist English learners in understanding vocabulary. The read-aloud features available in many software programs are another example.

2. *Take steps to keep students safe.* Always supervise students' use of the internet and ensure responsive technology practices by providing explicit instruction in anti-bullying, identity protection, media literacy, and general internet safety practices as a prerequisite to students using the internet independently.

3. *Design classrooms and other school areas so that students can see teachers model the responsible use of technology.* With the internet now accessible in most U.S. classrooms, teachers have the obligation to ensure it's used constructively (Faison, 1996). While most districts have policies for acceptable use of the internet and computers, it is essential that teachers model and demonstrate responsible and ethical usage of the various technologies and social networks that are available.

4. *Pay attention to the physical space.* Ensure there is effective and appropriate lighting, enough room to work comfortably and ergonomically, and adjustable sound volume (including headphones).

We understand that many school districts cannot afford to make every technological advance available to students and that countless economically disadvantaged students do not have access to tech resources at home. The digital divide between students in low- versus middle- and high-income schools is a national dilemma (Anderson, 2016) and must be remedied so there is equitable access for all students. It is also a challenge in rural areas. Some rural schools are attempting to remedy the divide by working closely with their public libraries to ensure that their students have access to high-speed internet and technology. Microsoft is also seeking innovative ways to bring the internet to the homes of rural students by turning buses "into internet-enabled hotspots" (Fung, 2018). As we seek solutions to the digital divide, the goal of supporting the classroom design with the infusion of technology is an essential component to our goal of empowering learners.

* * * * *

The next chapter examines classroom-based experiences that support students' continuous development of planning and organizing skills, time management, maintaining focus amid sensory stimulation, detail retention, social cuing, and the ability to complete multistep tasks. We look at ways that teachers can strengthen students' capacities—differentiating based on each student's unique needs—to develop and exercise these skills. We also provide classroom-based extensions that give students the opportunity to practice this learning through real-world applications.

Self-Directed Learning
and Positive Interdependence

Each student in K–12 public schools in the United States is generally one of about 20 or 30 young people in his or her classroom. Every student is expected to enact a broad array of positive behaviors and dispositions. For example, they are expected to show persistence, even when they are challenged. They are expected to recognize when they need support and know how to ask for it; to follow rules, take direction, and think independently; to express their point of view; and to be collaborative, taking into account the ideas, contributions, and questions of others. Further, they are expected to practice all of these behaviors and dispositions while also successfully completing a semester filled with mandated curricular learning and tasks. It's a lot.

It's been said that "Those who have a *why* can bear with almost any *how*." In this chapter, we provide a framework for helping students find the why they need to rise to their many challenges and pursue all they are expected to do. Motivation, we argue, is powered by specific dispositions and behaviors that strengthen students' sense of personal control, increase their feelings of competence, and enhance their abilities to contribute to the classroom community. We'll delve into the following topics:

- **Helping students see learning as a positive experience.** This means creating activities that allow students to leverage their strengths and use these strengths to succeed. But it also means taking into account how the brain learns and factoring in the powerful role of emotion.
- **Fostering and establishing zones for deep learning.** Students can find relevance in tasks that build their capacity and boost their confidence.
- **Building students' confidence in themselves as independent learners.** This work involves creating the expectation of success, digging deeply into students' personal motivations, and providing support for key skills and dispositions.
- **Modeling unconditional acceptance.** This is a way to honor, value, acknowledge, and support every student.
- **Building interdependence in a community of trust.** When we do this, we enhance our students' sense of safety, ability to concentrate, and positive attitude toward learning.

Helping Students See Learning Positively

To be human is to experience conflicting impulses that battle for dominance. For example, what makes some students embrace a challenge and others flee from it? For that matter, what makes some students come to class enthusiastic to learn while others would rather be anywhere else? We all have experienced having an impulse to act out of anger or run away, often without regard for future consequences. Yet, as adults, we somehow (usually) find ways to prevent the ill-considered reactions or impulses that would otherwise overtake us.

 Time for Reflection

Think about a challenging experience you had in the past few years and answer these questions:

- What fight-or-flight actions could you have taken that you chose not to take?
- What did you do to stop yourself from engaging in those impulsive behaviors?

As children mature, they begin to take into account others' feelings, thoughts, and ideas as well as their own. Their actions are tempered by a more nuanced understanding of the self, the world, and others. While we might attribute this maturation to the simple accumulation of experiences, it's better explained by the highly malleable nature of the human brain. With this in mind, we'd like to dig a little deeper into how the brain functions in classroom and school environments and relate that to what we can do with and for our students to enhance or inhibit these developmental processes.

According to James E. Zull (2004), a professor of biology and biochemistry and the director of the Center for Innovation in Teaching and Education, learning depends on two critical elements: *practice* and *emotion*.

Take a Closer Look: The Role of Practice and Emotion in Learning

With friends coming over for a special meal, we decide to make a dessert that we have never made before: baklava, a multilayered pastry filled with chopped walnuts and a honey-infused syrup. The first step of the recipe calls for us to lay out a single layer of filo dough, paint it with melted butter, and repeat the process six more times. On the first try, the first layer of filo dough crumbles into a sorry mess of broken pieces. We pause and seek advice on baklava making from a friend and the internet. Buoyed by encouragement and tips, we lay out another layer of filo, paint it with butter, and experience the same problem: the filo layer continues to break apart. We take a breath, review the steps and tips, and try again. After a lot of trial and error and persistence, we finally have a facsimile of our chosen dessert and are ready to bake it. It comes out too dry. So we try the whole process again. A few hours later, finally and gratefully, we create what we call a confectionary wonder. We serve the baklava to our friends, who reward us with so many compliments that we vow to make baklava our signature dessert.

Let's use a neuroscientific lens to consider the steps we took to move from a novice baklava maker to an experienced one. Practicing new skills by engaging in a process of trial and error actually changes the brain. With each bit of sensory information and each thought, neurons form branching interconnections to other neurons, building an ever-growing network of synapses (Zull, 2004). In this example, every time we tried to make the baklava, we created additional connections among the growing thoughts, impressions, and memories that relate to what it is to make baklava (the concept) *and* how to do it (the process). Each time we tried again, we built additional understanding. Ultimately, we succeeded in the task through persistence and were praised for the outcome, reinforcing our sense that sticking to a task pays off.

Zull (2004, 2011) explains that for learning to occur, in addition to practice and effort, there must be an experience that activates an emotional biochemical reaction that triggers a neurophysiological response in the brain. This reaction greatly influences our learning *and* our outcome. For example, let's say that our first attempt to make the baklava is so negative that it releases so much cortisol in our bloodstream that we experience an aversion to ever repeating the attempt. Our negative learning experience is so powerful that it affects our beliefs and behavior. We might then say to our friends, "I tried to make baklava, and I will never, *ever* do that again."

In response to emotional events, the brain releases a lot of different chemicals, among them adrenaline, dopamine, and serotonin, which help create the biochemical basis for the positive and negative reactions we "feel" in response to positive or negative experiences. All this explains why a key part of educators' mission must be helping students experience learning as positive. We can do so by working to ensure students feel safe, a sense of belonging, acknowledgment, and competence as they learn. And this requires that we continuously help them see their strengths and capacities, which is only possible when we create activities that are meaningful to them and that are properly attuned to their current capacities so that they may create their own ideas—activities that, according to Zull (2004), are created through students' *positive emotions*.

Establishing and Fostering Zones Where Deep Learning Can Occur

Students' wholehearted commitment to learning requires more than a sense of belonging, although the sense of having people support you in your failures and your successes is an invaluable foundation to being emotionally available to concentrate on complex tasks. Studies that map brain structures, levels of dopamine, and other essential chemical transmitters during learning experiences show evidence of both the harmful effects of stress and the positive effects of relaxation on the brain's ability to process and retain information (Willis, 2014). If we want students to learn deeply, we must work to make them feel safe, connected, and competent.

The type of deep learning that we are describing requires cultivation of a host of positive conditions. One is an environment that supports students' commitment to learning. This starts with creating the conditions students need to connect lesson content to something that matters to them. It requires that we provide materials, tasks, and activities that relate in some way to students' interests and experiences. For example, a high school biology teacher who works in a coastal fishing community, where most students' families work either directly in the fishing industry or in professions that support it, might create units that explore the challenges of invasive species and how their effects might be remedied. By presenting content from the biology standards and the course text in a manner that is personally, socially, and culturally meaningful to students, the teacher creates positive conditions for learning.

It's also important that learning tasks and activities be developmentally appropriate. In her book *Understanding How Young Children Learn,* Wendy L. Ostroff (2012) shares some critical insight from development expert John Locke:

> Infants and children do not set out to learn any of the vast repertoire of skills that they gain in the first years. Instead, they study the faces, voices, and actions of others out of a deep biological need for emotional interaction with those who love and care for them. They simply find themselves in a social and cultural context that values certain skills and uses them constantly. Learning, then, is an unintended bonus. (pp. 7–8)

As children mature to the age of 6 or 7 years old, they develop more curiosity, questions, abilities, and interests in socializing and interacting with peers (Erikson & Erikson, 1998). They also become more focused on thinking independently and seeking intellectual or aesthetic rewards in tasks. Cultivation of such self-motivated learning is at the heart of educational approaches like Montessori, where even early childhood classrooms feature objects from nature; a calming, uncluttered openness; and a sense of order (Lillard, 2005). What such order communicates to a child is an optimistic sense that a complex world may be understood by one's own effort. From there, the novel, diverse, and often unpredictable phenomena of a child's world can begin to be classified, anticipated, and brought into familiarity by learners exercising their own curiosity and efforts.

During the preteen and teen years, motivation becomes increasingly linked to peer relationships and the quest to explore one's personal identity. Children at these stages of development are increasingly drawn to learning with and from peers, even as they deepen their capacity for introspection, reflection, and autonomous engagement with learning tasks. Some older students may find themselves motivated by their desire to engage with others to find friendships and to learn about who they are as social beings (Erikson & Erikson, 1998). Many older students find deeper positive meaning and motivation by asking themselves questions such as these:

- Is what I'm learning relevant to something I care about?
- Will knowing this, or being able to do this, open doors for me and help me become a more capable, empowered person?
- Does engaging with this content give me intellectual or aesthetic pleasure or a sense of empowerment?

Each of these questions suggests a strategy we might use to foster a zone of deep learning.

Help students find relevance. The art of teaching involves the ability to find, feel, and offer to students these kinds of connections with a sense of enthusiasm or sincere appreciation for their value. We recall the example of a 4th grader who had difficulty finding motivation for learning to read. The student was several years behind the expected reading level and was resistant to doing reading work at home. Her self-perceived lack of progress discouraged her from working to develop her skills. But when her best friend moved away, she expressed an urgent need to stay in touch with her using text messages. With her teacher's wholehearted encouragement to communicate with her friend, she produced a quantum leap in her literacy skills in a few short months. The moral of this anecdote: seeing the relevance of learning something is a surprisingly powerful motivator to overcome learning obstacles.

Ask big questions for students to answer. Human beings share a universal, intrinsic drive to seek patterns and answers to great and profound mysteries. The Big History Project (Sorkin, 2014) draws on the power of this human search for meaning as the basis for an interdisciplinary exploration of online resources designed for middle and high school students. It features video lectures, slideshows, and activities that trace the origin of modern humans, beginning with the big bang and the formation of stars and planets through to the formation of Earth and the natural history and human history of our world.

Offer calibrated challenge to build capacity and confidence. Watching young people (or similarly motivated adults) play and master video games, it is apparent that the pleasure of meeting a steep but not impossible challenge can be energizing and motivating. The satisfaction of a self-selected "just right" challenge, with its implications for education, was brought to popular attention by Mihaly Csikszentmihalyi (1990) with his concept of *flow*. The terms *flow state* and *in the zone* are used interchangeably to describe an immersive activity in which a person feels completely absorbed, energized, focused, and involved. Video game designer Jane McGonigal (2011) applied this definition to the state that young people experience when playing video games and the possibilities of using these gaming techniques to activate and empower students' learning: "A game is an opportunity to focus our energy, with relentless optimism, at something we're good at (or getting better at) and enjoy" (location no. 542).

Sixth grade teacher Kevin Hodgson shows us the possibilities that were realized when he made video games a part of his students' learning experience. He serendipitously learned about his students' interests in video games as the class was waiting for the dismissal announcements at the end of the day.

 ### Take a Closer Look: The Role Video Games Can Play in Learning

The end of the school day is the perfect time for eavesdropping. We wait in our classroom for the dismissal announcements, chatting casually. My 6th graders are more open in their conversations, letting their guard down a bit more than usual. It was here that I first started to understand the role that video games were playing in their lives outside school.

I wondered how I could capture the excitement I was hearing in their voices to teach them about the power of writing. It felt like an opportunity. I began to do my research. Thanks to connections within the National

Writing Project, I came across the perfect platform: Gamestar Mechanic. It is constructed to teach young people how to design, build, and publish video games. This online site has become a key piece in bringing video games into my English language arts classroom. In doing so, I have been able to expand our learning of what composition is and what story is by fully integrating design and writing into a project that ends with a student-created video game published in a space where thousands of other peer users around the world also play.

The reaction of students when I tell them that we are going to be designing and publishing video games in school is priceless. They can't quite believe it; it's as if we are breaking some rules of learning. And when they first enter Gamestar, they are intrigued by the possibilities and excited to get started.

My 6th graders have built science-based video games (using cell mitosis and layers of Earth as framing devices, in partnership with our science teacher), mythological games (based on Greek stories of old, in collaboration with our social studies teacher), and math games (teaching the order of operations in a mathematical expression). In the past few years, they have published adventure story/games on a Hero's Journey template. What began as casual conversation on the bus line now is a central part of my writing curriculum each winter. So I keep listening. You never know what you might hear.

—Kevin Hodgson, 6th grade teacher, technology liaison with the Western Massachusetts Writing Project, Southampton, Massachusetts

 Time for Reflection

1. Describe two ways that you believe the video game activities in Kevin Hodgson's classroom established and fostered zones where deep learning could occur.
2. How might you apply similar ideas to your own work?

Building Students' Confidence in Themselves as Independent Learners

Success breeds success. Creating appealing and effective learning tasks for our diverse students involves locating and sharing our own enthusiasms and positive associations with learning. It also calls for us to take into account our insights and awareness about our students in order to create meaningful and motivating tasks for them. And we have to foster conditions that allow students to expect positive outcomes and achieve them (see Figure 4.1). Let's delve into these challenges.

FIGURE 4.1

Fostering a Culture of Interconnected and Interdependent Awareness

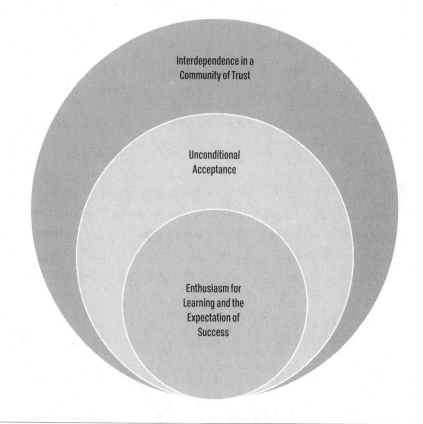

Interdependence in a
Community of Trust

Unconditional
Acceptance

Enthusiasm for
Learning and the
Expectation of
Success

Creating the Expectation of Positive Outcomes

Returning to the baklava-making example and some of the neuroscience research helps us explain what we mean by "expecting positive outcomes." The baklava story illustrates a successful experience, one in which we wanted a positive outcome so much that we hung in, thought through the challenge, stayed focused, used our investigative powers to find solutions to the problems that we experienced along the way, and were adventurous in trying to make something we had not made before. All of these positive dispositions could have been overtaken by negative impulses that might have resulted in our doubting ourselves, giving up, feeling like a failure, fearing our capacity to think creatively, and more (see Figure 4.2).

FIGURE 4.2

Positive and Negative Dispositions for Learning

Positive Disposition	Negative Disposition
Persistence	Giving up easily
Creativity	Doubting creative competence
Willingness to take risks	Fear of taking risks
Confidence	Self-doubt

What made the difference in the baklava example is that our expectation of a positive outcome held from start to finish. That positive dispositional expectation led to enough of a state of calm and persistence that our brain's chemistry supported our drive to be successful. Our example can be readily applied to what we want students to feel in classroom settings: that a positive outcome will occur for each of them.

 Time for Reflection

Choose an activity that you feel able to take risks in, such as taking a beginner's class in a new skill, trying a new food at a restaurant, or implementing a new strategy in your teaching. Identify two to three experiences you have had that may have contributed to your sense of capability.

Creating a Safe Environment for Independent and Collaborative Learning

The process of becoming an empowered, confident, and competent learner requires that students have multiple practice opportunities—what we call *space*—to think, plan, organize, and work independently and creatively. They also need exposure to the range of ideas, contributions, and questions that come from learning and socializing with others, and they need freedom to make the inevitable mistakes that are a part of learning. Accordingly, teachers need to provide opportunities for students to engage in both independent and collaborative tasks.

Students' exploration and studies demand that we take many actions that provide them with the space and tools needed to practice using the academic and social-emotional skills that will help them succeed autonomously and collaboratively. We want all students to feel relaxed, safe, and connected to the content they are learning as well as the community in which they are learning so that they can enter—consciously and subconsciously—the relaxed calm state that facilitates learning.

In the previous section, we looked at some of the physiological responses that occur when we have positive and negative dispositions. Stephen Porges (2011) describes the two responses as being prosocial versus defensive. In classroom settings, whether students are working on their own, as a whole class, or in pairs and small groups, we must take actions that will help them work together, learn together, socialize, and even bond.

Taking Action to Support Cooperation and Self-Reliance

We know that that establishing and maintaining a harmonious collaborative environment that supports both cooperation and self-reliance almost always requires direct teaching and deliberate guidance. As noted in Chapter 1, we believe that student empowerment is only possible when students feel safe and feel a sense of belonging. We have identified five principles teachers can follow when designing classroom learning activities that will help achieve these ends.

Promote care. To be truly empowered, humans are deeply dependent on the cooperation of everyone around them to be self-aware while simultaneously being aware of others. A first step is to explicitly co-create an environment in which each student knows they are cared for and about by their teacher, peers, and others in the classroom. For example, before engaging his 5th grade students in a series of science experiments that they would carry out in small groups, veteran teacher Roger Gibbons invested time in team-building and partner-skills activities and emphasized creating a caring environment where everyone feels that they are safe, that they belong, and that they can be successful.

Prioritize emotional safety. The responsibility for creating an emotionally safe environment begins with the adults in the classroom, but it cannot be imparted or imposed effectively by them exclusively. Ultimately, the emotional safety of a classroom community is co-created by students and teachers who are willing to communicate openly about feelings and needs to find satisfying resolutions to challenges and problems.

Provide structure. Structure plays an important role in students developing the positive dispositions of persistence, creativity, willingness to take risks, and confidence. We use the word *structure* in reference to the system of explicitly organized actions teachers take in the classroom. It's another way of describing the collection of strategies that teachers employ to create order and ensure students have appealing opportunities to leverage their strengths and practice using new ideas. Among the structures that Roger Gibbons uses are holding science class at the same time every day and expecting everyone to bring their science text and notebooks to class, sit in their small groups, walk quietly from their classroom into the school courtyard to conduct their experiments, and work collaboratively as a group to note their observations.

Creating a classroom structure supports students' continuous development of important skills like planning and organizing tasks, managing time, focusing attention on particular tasks and procedures, sticking with a task through completion, retaining details, engaging in interactional tasks that rely on social cuing, and following a sequence of tasks. These sets of routinely occurring actions give students many opportunities to regulate their individual and collective actions. As creativity expert Julia Cameron has observed, structures provide a sense of safety that makes risk taking more feasible: "In limits there is freedom. Creativity thrives within structure. Creating safe havens where our children are allowed to dream, play, make a mess and, yes, clean it up, we teach them respect for themselves and others" (Groskop, 2013, para. 14). Figure 4.3 shows a variety of ways that teachers can foster the sense of structure students need to undertake complicated challenges.

FIGURE 4.3

Structure-Providing Strategies to Build Self-Direction Skills

Skills	Strategies for Grades K–2	Strategies for Grades 3–5	Strategies for Grades 6–12
Planning and organizing tasks	"Think aloud" and rehearse as you model your own process for completing a task that students will undertake, and begin to organize students' work using emerging literacy strategies, such as stickers and pictures.	"Think aloud" and model processes; organize students' work in a calendar planner, using more sophisticated schedules and planners with due dates for older students.	
Managing time	Have visual timers that show the remaining time until a transition. Give older students responsibility for documenting their work periods in a written organizer and making written plans or summaries of their accomplishments.		Conference with students about their work goals and their progress, prompting them to reflect on what is going well and how they might address challenges.
Listening and focusing	Teach listening and focus skills through controlled breathing, yoga and movement, listening games, and the use of physical response (e.g., nodding, giving a thumbs-up or thumbs-down). Encourage students to observe nature and natural objects. Sample activities: – Incorporate periods of quiet into the daily routine. (Primary) – Help students notice how their sensory and physical needs affect their attention, and show them ways to mediate the effects. (Elementary)		In addition to teaching controlled breathing, yoga, and movement, offer technology supports such as audio readers and writing on computers. Sample activities: –Vary methods of presentation. –Incorporate breaks and movement.
Choosing and using appropriate tools to support focus	Help students become aware of sensory stimuli that they can modify, and provide tools like noise-canceling headphones, movement or exercise breaks, preferred seating, fidget spinners, and cushioned seats that they can use to avoid distraction.		
Retaining details	Provide multisensory experiences that help link information to as many different senses as possible.	Use music, art, making/creating things, and physical experiences in daily instruction. Have students work with a partner and reflect on lessons' key ideas and insights.	Provide students with opportunities to teach what they've learned to peers. Teach them how sleep, hydration, and proper nutrition optimize the brain's ability to learn.
Engaging in interactive tasks that rely on social cuing	Explicitly teach and have students practice taking turns, being a good listener, making eye contact, and supporting a speaker through good listening.	Explicitly teach and have students practice the skills of cooperative learning. Discuss and rehearse the challenges of the process of working together and generate a collaborative set of guidelines for how to make such interactions successful.	

(continued)

FIGURE 4.3 (cont.)

Structure-Providing Strategies to Build Self-Direction Skills

Skills	Strategies for Grades K–2	Strategies for Grades 3–5	Strategies for Grades 6–12
Executing a sequence or series of tasks	Play memory games such as "I'm Going on a Picnic," where each new player summarizes the previous players' contributions. Teach and lead songs that have built-up verses, such as "I Know an Old Lady Who Swallowed a Fly" to promote memory.	Provide visual and written summaries of multistep directions on classroom signage and on the paperwork provided to students.	Encourage students to create written or visual summaries of concepts or processes they are studying, including flow charts, posters, and digital presentations. Have them practice the skills of reducing, synthesizing, or simplifying information to essentials.

Provide predictability. Routines and practices that are consistent and predictable are critical for learning. This includes having predictable daily schedules and a routine flow to lesson sequences. In practice, students might routinely gather as a whole class at the beginning of a lesson, then separate into pairs, then in small groups, and end each class back as a whole group. Predictability that students can count on is critical. This includes teachers taking time to support them as they transition from one activity to the next. According to clinical psychologist Margaret Blaustein (2013), director of the Trauma Training and Education Division at the Justice Resource Institute, predictability supports students' brains in achieving a calm and positive state in which learning can occur. We can find an example of this type of predictability in Roger Gibbons's approach to handling transitions in his classroom. Rather than leaving this to chance, he gives his students explicit information and guidance as they transition from a whole-class to a small-group or paired activity, modeling what he wants students to do in terms of the tasks they engage in and the types of positive behaviors they enact with each other.

Provide practice adapting to change. When all of the preceding conditions are present in a classroom environment, everyone has an expectation that the classroom is a safe and nurturing place. And change is far easier to cope with than unpredictability. Good teachers know the unpredictable nature of a school environment. They are aware of the unpredictable nature of important circumstances such as fire and safety drills as well as the inevitability of unforeseen circumstances of students' lives. They explicitly provide students with supports about what to do when such circumstances arise. For example, they explain and provide practice for drills before they occur so that students are ready for them. They also provide practice opportunities for students to support one another when an unpredictable event happens to someone.

Modeling and Encouraging Unconditional Acceptance

An example of the power of unconditional acceptance can be found in Liz Murray's best-selling memoir *Breaking Night* (2006), when she writes about the care teachers provided her throughout her childhood when her family's homelessness meant she was in and out of the foster care system. Decades of research affirm the critical importance of acceptance.

Norma Gonzalez, Luis C. Moll, and Cathy Amanti (2005), expert scholars and researchers in equity, linguistics, and diversity, coined the term *funds of knowledge* to describe the many strengths and assets that all people possess and documented how important it is for educators to honor, acknowledge, and value the diverse members of their learning communities. In addition, the tenets of positive psychology focus on the infinite possibilities that can be accomplished when we believe in people's capacity to work with, value, and support one another (Maslow, 1987). While we know this to be true, especially as it applies to individuals and groups who may perceive themselves as having less status and value than others (Cohen & Lotan, 2014), it is critical that we seek effective ways to encourage unconditional acceptance among everyone in our classroom and school community.

One of the most important things we can do in this area is support each student's ability to see their own strengths and competencies and those of their peers, and then help them engage in interactions that meaningfully demonstrate these positives. Let's look at an exchange that occurred in Michael's 2nd grade class after he asked the class to clean up the room, and one student objected, blurting out, "I didn't make that mess!"

Stephanie: Yeah, I didn't make a mess, and I hate cleaning up after Alexa. She is so messy.

Tony: Yeah, and Max can't help us cause he's in a wheelchair!

Mr. Silverstone: I feel sad when I hear that we might not want our class-room tidy, and I believe that all of us are quite capable to make it a space that is ours. Let's come together on our rug and discuss how we might make the classroom a physical space that works for all of us.

 Time for Reflection

Describe two or three subsequent interactions that Michael might have to support his students' ability to perceive their peers positively and use expressions to show their unconditional acceptance.

Humanist psychologist Carl Rogers (1956) pioneered the idea of being person centered by having empathy and unconditional acceptance toward others. Since he first presented this idea, a growing body of research in a variety of areas has demonstrated the value of unconditional acceptance. This includes research findings in psychotherapy and positive psychology (Seligman, Rashid, & Parks, 2006), positive youth development (Floyd & McKenna, 2003; Lerner, Almerigi, Theokas, & Lerner, 2005), and education (Biswas-Dienera, Kashdan, & Gurpal, 2011; Gonzalez et al., 2005; Steele, 2010). These studies show how important it is for adults and children to take time to find the strengths that are in all of us, including ourselves. Understandably, this might seem like an impossible task when we are confronted with someone whom we perceive as smarter, more athletic, or more creative than us, or someone whom we perceive to be less smart, less athletic, or less creative.

Deficit-based perspectives such as these have been shown to have a deleterious effect on students' academic and social-emotional outcomes, especially students in a racial, economic, cultural, linguistic, ethnic, or gender group that is perceived negatively (Steele, 2010). A hypothetical example of the kind of deficit-based thinking that Steele presents is the notion that children who use wheelchairs should not be involved in cleaning up a classroom because they have a disability. Let's say that a teacher or student embraces this deficit-based way of thinking. How is that thinking expressed to peers, teachers, and others? And, just as important, what does that type of negative thinking and expression about it mean to the student who uses the wheelchair? According to Steele, these negative perceptions can have a powerfully negative impact. If we push our example a bit further, let's consider a student who uses a wheelchair who sees this difference as something that prevents her from being a full member of her classroom community. She wonders, "Because of my chair, will I always be the last one picked?"

Negative perceptions and expressions can lead each of us to think negatively about others and ourselves, and they can hamper or even squelch our ability to see our own potential and the potential in others. In other words, unconditional acceptance in a classroom setting involves some important requisites: (1) that we feel a sense of safety, belonging, acknowledgment, and competence; and (2) that we want everyone to feel the same. There are two valuable questions that can help guide us in achieving these requisites.

1. *Am I a member no matter what?* Think back to our student who uses a wheelchair and perceives that she will always be the last one picked because of her disability. In a secure environment of unconditional acceptance, she might share these fears with her classmates and teacher. When we and our students ask this question, we consider our place within the whole, reflect on our values, and consider what we owe to our community and what our community might do to support each of us.

2. *Will I be accepted regardless of my circumstances?* This is a question that prompts us to be mindful of the various and changing circumstances that may arise. As an example, think about a student whose father is detained by immigration officials. This student's distress might lead him to display a variety of emotions in class, from an unwillingness or inability to engage with others to being unpredictably aggressive to others. When we encourage students to reflect on this question, it supports our goal of encouraging unconditional acceptance. It is also helpful in building an interdependent community of trust—our next topic of discussion.

Building Interdependence in a Community of Trust

As we help students develop the ability to self-direct their work and navigate a complex social environment, there is only so much that we—and they—can accomplish as individuals. The myth of individual success for a fortunate few *over* others, which permeates so many aspects of thinking about business, higher education, and many other areas of society, is a destructive model for a classroom. What's essential for learners is an interdependent environment of trust in which a lowered sense of threat coupled with a higher sense of confidence free up students' capacity to concentrate, to imagine, and to experience a sense of safety within initial uncertainty. As educators, we can support such an environment through our intentions and our actions.

Social psychologists David McMillan and David Chavis (1986) identified the foundations of a sense of community as "a feeling that members have of belonging, a feeling that members matter to one another and to the group, and a shared faith that members' needs will be met through their commitment to be together" (p. 9). To create a sense of belonging requires a commitment from educators to see classroom community as a necessary component of learning and the participants to be interdependent on each other for its success.

What might this look like in practice?

In an elementary classroom, it might be a morning gathering to share a greeting and for children to share experiences from their lives so that they may come to know each other, be known, and find commonalities with each other. Beginning the day with the entire class gathered to say each other's names aloud, to play a game, or to share an interest or special event in their lives creates an environment where students can feel that they belong and matter to others.

In middle and high school, trust might be more effectively developed at the peer level, through group and partner work where working together to complete an assignment means that learners rely on each other for their perspectives and efforts. Regardless of the subject being taught, having room to develop partnership and team skills by sharing unique interests, preferences, and skills allows students to experience a sense that each member of the group has something to contribute and that this contribution matters and is valued.

No matter the setting, the educator contributes to the creation of a community of trust by showing genuine interest and curiosity in students as people from the moment they enter the room by engaging them in conversation, asking how their weekend was, and listening to what they might want to share or ask. An example of this type of expressing interest and curiosity comes from teacher Sandra Deacon.

Take a Closer Look: Showing Genuine Interest and Caring

At our school, the children walk directly into their coatroom, so I greet them as they arrive, and we shake hands. I teach them how to do a firm handshake, because in our culture, that's a good thing for everyone to have.

Before class starts, I take a moment to check in with each student, making eye contact and saying, "Good morning" and "How are you doing?" In these moments we can have just a brief conversation, and usually [I can] tell if a student is tired, or if they are excited to be there, or if they are not feeling well. I think it teaches them grace and that they are being welcomed into our classroom, which is a community. That they are welcome and that we [the class community] are glad that they are here that day, especially if they have been sick or absent—it lets them know that they are noticed.

— Sandra Deacon, teacher, Avila, Indiana

An additional example of creating conditions conducive to positive outcomes, unconditional acceptance, and interdependence in a community of trust comes from Marta Donahoe, the director of professional development at the Cincinnati Montessori Secondary Teacher Education Program, who tells us about a two-week immersion course.

 Take a Closer Look: Positive Outcomes, Unconditional Acceptance, and Interdependence

Before heading out on a two-week immersion course with secondary students, we create two posted lists: "Hopes" and "Fears." These lists are important, because I'll want to know where to pause and where to move forward with the group. The stakes are high. We will be with one another for two weeks, all day, every day, and sometimes with overnights or camping in the woods. After we generate those two lists, I ask the class what agreements they think we need to make to be able to look at one another at the end of the course and feel like we all know and love one another.

Over the years, I've made dozens of lists with my students, and the same broad ideas are on every one: help one another be on time, see a need/fill a need, remind one another to be kind, celebrate our persistence and courage, collaborate on assignments, and be grateful.

We create a self-evaluation based on these agreements, and the students fill it out and turn it in each evening along with their reflective journal prompt, which I borrowed from Rachel Naomi Remen and is always the same: *What surprised me? What inspired me? What moved me?* We open community meeting in the mornings with each student reading her response to one of those questions. These simple structures create a soulfulness in the group, and at the end of the course, we always know and love one another.

—Marta Donohoe, director of professional development of the Cincinnati Montessori Secondary Teacher Education Program, Cincinnati, Ohio

Examples such as these show us how educators use time before, during, after, and between lessons to be curious, be observant about what students have to say, make inferences about how students may be feeling and why, and learn about the circumstances of their lives and the things that are important to them that make them who they are. Teachers have a job to do, which is ostensibly to convey information and skills, but beyond (and including) the role of classroom manager, it is essential to create a relationship that has an unconditional quality to it. We care about our students not only because they are learners in our classroom, but also because they inspire our curiosity, respect, and affection as human beings.

The more students know how naturally curious and caring the adults in the room are, and the more firmly established the classroom ethos of care, responsiveness, and honesty is, the richer the conditions are for students to develop trust in themselves and others. Ultimately, this trust reverberates in many actions among students and is self-reinforcing. We trust because we are trusted. We act in dependable ways and know we can depend on others. We don't fear the inevitable imperfection and vulnerabilities involved in learning, and we are willing to venture into new and unfamiliar learning when the trust in the community tells us it is socially safe to do so. We are empowered.

For an example of the power of a teacher demonstrating genuine interest and care, we offer the experience of an elementary school teacher in North Carolina and a student of hers who enrolled in her classroom six weeks after the school year had begun. This teacher always ate lunch with her class, and during this student's first few weeks of school, she asked him to sit next to her so that they could interact on a personal level. Here's the story she shared with us:

> Earlier that week, he had met an academic goal, and I told him, "I am just so proud of you. You know I care about you, right?" And he looked down and whispered, "Yes." And then I said, "Well, how do you know that?" And he said, "Well, I think about it." And I said, "Well, when do you think about it?" And he said, "I think about it every morning on the way to school." For me, that was a real window to look through and know that he knows that our relationship is really important. Until we reached that point of him knowing that we care, his learning was kind of stagnant. The relationship that we have built has really propelled his desire to learn and to work harder.

 Time for Reflection

1. Describe an experience you had with a student in which your goal was to foster interdependence in a community of trust through relationship building.
2. Consider some ways that you might alter your classroom procedures to provide opportunities to build interdependence in a community of trust.

* * * * *

In the next chapter, we examine how we can support students' work to develop the skills, understandings, and abilities to engage in self-reflection and confidently navigate different fields of knowledge, cultures, and social interactions. We also show how to support students in feeling safe to make approximations (and errors) as they learn.

Student Self-Reflection

It was the end of the day for Ms. Foster's 3rd graders—time for classroom clean-up. But rather than participate in the clean-up work, Timothy stayed in his seat, still making an origami bird. His classmate, Maribel, did not like this at all. After angrily demanding that Timothy put the bird away and join in, she called him lazy, stomped her feet, and stormed off in a huff.

Ms. Foster was watching from a short distance. She approached Maribel and said, "You seem angry. Let's step outside so I can help you in private."

"I didn't do anything!" Maribel protested, accompanying Ms. Foster into the hallway. "I always get in trouble! Timothy's a baby. He won't listen, and I hate him!"

"Wow, I can see how much it frustrates you when people don't do their part or listen," Ms. Foster responded.

"Yes!" Maribel agreed. "Everybody's supposed to help, and he isn't helping, and I told him he had to, and he just ignored me."

"I get frustrated with that too," Ms. Foster said. "Nobody likes being ignored."

Maribel's expression melted a little from anger to sadness.

"Are you open to some advice?" Ms. Foster asked. Taking Maribel's silence as a willingness to listen, she continued, "When someone tells me to do something in an angry way, even if I know I am *supposed* to do it, I'm less likely to want to do it. That's true for everyone; that's just the way people are. But if I get asked or reminded to do something in a kind way, or even a regular way, I'm more likely to do it. It doesn't mean I *will*; it just means I can think about doing it without wanting to fight back. Can you practice with me? Pretend I'm Timothy and ask me to join in the clean-up. But say it without being mad. Tell him why it matters to you and ask if he would be willing to help. Why *does* it matter to you that he cleans up?'"

"Because it's not fair if only some people help," Maribel said.

"OK, without being mad, can you say, 'Timothy, it's not fair if only some people help. Would you be willing to help too?'"

"Timothy! It's not fair—"

Ms. Foster broke in gently, "Try saying it calmly, like you are trying to get him to understand."

"Timothy . . . it's not fair if—"

"That's going to work so much better, Maribel," Ms. Foster said encouragingly.

"Timothy, it's not fair if only some people help," Maribel said. "Could you help too?"

"That's it, that's it, Maribel! Try it that way. Would you like me to stand there with you?"

They returned to the classroom, and Maribel approached Timothy again. To her surprise (but not Ms. Foster's), the neutral request worked. In a private moment the next day, Ms. Foster invited Maribel to reflect on how her second effort with Timothy was more effective than her first. What did she do differently the second time? Why did those changes matter?

We turn now to the topic of what teachers can do to help students develop the skills and habit of self-reflection, which they need to confidently navigate different types of knowledge, different sets of cultural expectations, and—as with Maribel and Timothy—all kinds of social interactions. Specifically, we'll investigate the following topics:

- **The necessary work of affirming each student's cultural identity.**
  Identity plays an essential role in each person's learning.

- **Ways to create a mistake-safe culture.** Making errors is a fundamental necessity for learning, and understanding this frees students to explore and take risks.
- **How to infuse reflection into classroom practice.** Doing so helps students expand their individual repertoire of expertise; see themselves as confident, capable learners and community members; and set their own goals.
- **Ways to use self-assessment tools.** Journaling and similar techniques help students monitor their own academic and social growth.

Affirming Each Student's Identity

Let's look in on another exchange, this time between a kindergarten student and his teacher.

> **Mrs. Sanbourn:** Jason, do you know if you brought a drink in your lunchbox?
>
> **Jason:** It be at my grandma's.
>
> **Mrs. Sanbourn:** OK, your drink is at home with Grandma?
>
> **Jason:** Yes. She not home, she be at work.
>
> **Mrs. Sanbourn:** Well, you need a drink, then. We have orange juice and apple juice. Which would you like?
>
> **Jason:** Apple juice, please.
>
> **Mrs. Sanbourn:** Apple juice it is, Jason. You are so polite. I really appreciate the way you always say please and thank you. That is so thoughtful of you!

This exchange is one we often share in our work with educators. We follow up by asking them to reflect on (1) what this exchange reveals about Jason and (2) other ways his teachers might have responded. The replies we get suggest that the expressive flexibility that we encourage wholeheartedly with toddlers who are learning to speak doesn't always extend to school-aged children. For example, many educators have responded to the first question by using deficit-based descriptors of Jason, such as "He speaks so poorly." Responses to the second question often include comments that Jason's teacher should have corrected his grammar. One teacher, for example, suggested that Mrs. Sanbourn say, "Jason, you should say that the juice *is* at your grandmother's. We don't say *it be* at school. Here is what that looks like when I say it: *The juice is at my grandmother's. She is at work."* This may be admirable modeling, but it illustrates a too-common problem: how focusing on the ways in which students' self-expression deviates from teachers' cultural norms and "expected standards" causes us to miss valuable opportunities to promote student empowerment.

Why the Identity Students Bring Matters

There's no question that students' identity plays an enormous role in how they see themselves and how they approach learning. However, as educators, we tend to privilege a particular set of norms and behaviors over all others (LeMoine & Soto, 2016). As an example, we often make the mistake of considering the academic language or literacy associated with success in school to be the *only* language of value (Zacarian, 2013). Jason is a case in point. When he spoke with his teacher, he used the infinitive of the irregular verb *be*. According to renowned sociolinguist William Labov (2006), the unchanging or invariant form of this verb is commonplace in African American dialect and took root well over a century ago. As such, Jason is speaking in a way that reflects a source of strength in his life: his African American cultural heritage and his present-day community.

While fluency in academic language and literacy is important, and its development is a rightful instructional objective, prioritizing academic language as essentially "better" than all other forms of language is short-sighted, even harmful. Doing so does more than just devalue the richness of vernacular language; it risks communicating to students that the way their families and the community members speak is without value, and that the voice that they hear in their own mind, shaped and modeled by the people who matter most to them in the world, is "lesser than" or wrong.

The Role of Culturally Responsive Practices

A key way to convey respect for the unique and diverse identities of our students is by using culturally responsive teaching practices, which connect what we want our students to learn and their personal, social, cultural, language, and real-world identities and experiences (Zacarian, 2013; Zacarian & Silverstone, 2015; Zacarian & Soto, 2020).

As an example of the kind of connections that we are describing, consider the early elementary school teacher who asked her students to make and talk about "a flag of me." In this activity, students used construction paper and markers to depict various elements that make them who they are—family members, favorite foods, interests, hobbies, and so on. This teacher used a verbal literacy-focused task aligned with her curriculum as an opportunity for her students to learn more about their peers' identities and discuss what they have in common: grandparents as central figures in their lives, cultural heritage, a love of sports, and so on.

For a second example, consider the middle school teacher in a coastal community in Maine where most students' families work in the fishing industry. During a unit of study about marine biology, she discovered that many in the class knew a lot about what contributes to the health and well-being of the ocean ecosystem. She used their experience-grounded interest to establish a meaningful connection to the required curriculum.

Culturally responsive practices help students organize classroom content into a coherent and personally relevant narrative instead of viewing it as a random accumulation of isolated, impersonal, unrelated facts and experiences. Arthur Costa, the renowned educational scholar and founder of the Institute for Intellectual Behavior, reminds us that learning is an inescapably personal act that "must first be taken in through the senses, processed and understood, interiorized in the mind and body, and emotionally charged and acted upon" (2017, p. ix).

In Costa's definition, learning is a process of constructing meaning by taking in new information, examining it in relation to what we have already learned, and creating a new understanding. We deepen and expand these understandings by connecting them to other things we know, understand, and can do. As Kallick and Zmuda (2017) point out, teachers can guide this process in the classroom by purposefully engaging students in self-reflection. This means asking students questions they are interested in answering, posing problems they are motivated to solve, and encouraging them to be mindful of what they are learning, why they are learning, how they are learning, and what they might do to learn more effectively. When students engage in this work over time, they build a self-reflective habit of mind, and they can bring that mindset to a host of new challenges.

Bringing Students' Attention to Meaning Making

Jason's conversation with Mrs. Sanbourn provides an opportunity to look how a teacher might foster self-reflection even with very young students. Recall that

Mrs. Sanbourn asked Jason a question (if he had a drink in his lunchbox). His responses communicated that he *didn't* have a drink in his lunchbox, that the drink he would have brought to school was at home, and that his grandmother could not bring the forgotten drink to school because she was at work. Finally, he politely asked for apple juice. Jason's responses were deliberate and exact, and clearly conveyed that he understood the questions his teacher was asking. In addition, each of his responses provided Mrs. Sanbourn with plenty of information she could draw on to confirm *she* understood *him*. Drawing from what we have shared about building the self-reflective habit of mind, she might continue this conversation by affirming Jason, confirming his communication skills, and modeling making meaning through her own self-reflection. Here is one example of how she might go about it:

> Jason, I appreciate the information you shared with me about why your juice is at home. I know your grandma is busy at work and that we can't call her right now. Thank you for sharing that with me. You chose the apple juice. I'm curious to know if you like apple juice more than orange juice and why you do. Like, I like tea more than coffee because I like the smell of my breakfast tea, the rich tan color of it, and I like the way it warms me up. Coffee tastes more bitter to me, and I don't like it as much. How do you feel about apple juice and orange juice?

 Time for Reflection

1. Compare the response above to the teacher response we mentioned earlier: "Jason, you should say that the juice *is* at your grandmother's. We don't say *it be* at school." What adjectives would you use to describe the two different responses?
2. In what ways does the second response affirm Jason's identity and provide him with models of self-reflection and language?
3. What alternate language might you use to affirm Jason's identity and provide him with models of self-reflection and language?

Although Mrs. Sanbourn's response might seem overly formal and explanatory, the information it provides is exactly what is missing in the feedback that some teachers give to children. It is a detailed explanation of her thinking. Its explicitness provides insight into the complexity of her thoughts. She gives Jason a model of how to express thinking and then gives him the chance to use this model when she asks him to share some of the complexity of his thoughts with her. The art of teaching is communicating with students in ways that maintain a trusting rapport with them but also model new skills and encourage their use. Mrs. Sanbourn is prompting this kindergartner to reflect on how language is used, showing him how to use language in this new setting, and helping him expand his fluency in academic and social-emotional communication.

Creating a Mistake-Safe Culture

Mistakes are a necessary part of learning. They can highlight what we don't yet know or quite understand, and they can provide insight into how our knowledge and skills might be refined. Educational researchers Stefanie Rach, Stefan Ufer, and Aiso Heinze (2012) point out that many cultures worldwide have proverbs about the positives of making errors. For example, *even monkeys fall from trees* is a Korean proverb that casts mistakes as natural and inevitable rather than an indictment of those who make them (Ladner, 2018). This error-positive attitude is much more common than many of us might assume; to illustrate, our online search for the phrase *the value of making a mistake* yielded more than 170 million instant results.

Making errors provides an invaluable opportunity for students to receive feedback—which, when done in a safe environment, can empower students to be able to trust that making errors and getting feedback is a bridge to making better decisions and taking more skillful action. Further, just as dance studios have mirrors to help students visually confirm the precision of their movements, teacher and peer feedback helps learners develop awareness of the effectiveness of their communication.

One of the great challenges that educators face is knowing when to offer students guidance or correction and when to step back so that students have an opportunity to spot errors and make adjustments on their own or with peers. Another challenge is getting students to a place where they are willing to explore and learn from their mistakes openly and without fear of embarrassment or judgment. Students' sense of safety is key to meeting this second challenge.

In a study about the social psychology of errors and accidents in hospital settings, Edmondson (2004) identified the following as primary influencers on feeling safe:

- Being part of a culture that wholly values candid discussions of concerns, worries, and errors in order to become more conscious of how to reduce rather than hide them
- Working in an environment where leaders continuously foster a safe and nurturing environment for analyzing errors

Further, the research found that when participants were in this type of safe and trusting environment, they were far more likely to see errors as a means to develop and grow. We want to create the same nurturing and supportive environment recommended in Edmondson's (2004) research because we understand that learning is a process of trial and error. It involves taking risks and sometimes failing. We also understand that learning does not happen at a predictable pace. Sometimes we grasp new ideas quickly. Other times we plateau before we grow. And still other times, we get stuck.

When we do get stuck, one reason we tend to stay stuck is the fear of making a mistake. A good way to thwart this is to promote the value of making mistakes so that students see it is as essential for learning. A second strategy is to avoid using evaluative language about students' work without acknowledging their efforts and progress. An example of evaluative language use is a student arriving at the wrong quotient in a long division problem and being told just that the answer is wrong. Instead of the teacher taking time to walk through the steps the student took to arrive at that answer, perhaps pointing out instances of solid mathematical reasoning and prompting reexamination of where the student went off course, there's just a verdict: "Wrong." It's far too easy for a student to mistake this as a judgment of his or her worth or intelligence. What students need to keep moving forward (at a pace that works for them) is what Kallick and Zmuda (2017) and Curwin (2010) call a *mistake-safe culture*—one in which everyone agrees that errors are an inevitable and valuable part of learning.

We also want students to see their individual and collective errors as opportunities for growth. Further, it's possible to design elements in the work of learning that allow students to see that they have made an error without having to have it pointed out to them. For example, a teacher can allow students to spot their own errors by giving them the resources to do so—answer keys, or a sequence of tasks designed to lead students to self-correct. We also believe that teachers can design assignments in such a way that students can see that they have made an error without anyone having to point it out to them.

Let's look at an example from Mrs. Jameson's algebra class at a suburban high school, where students are studying variables for basic equations. Today, they are working in groups of four to practice some recently acquired problem-solving procedures. Mrs. Jameson begins the class by modeling aloud the steps she takes as she solves three different problem sets. Then, while solving a fourth set, she purposefully makes a mistake and begins thinking aloud about what she might do to remedy the error. She invites each small group to come up with possible corrections to her mistake. As they work, Mrs. Jameson walks among the groups, making comments such as "Remember to look for interesting mistakes to share later."

Each small group has several suggestions. They know that in this class, making mistakes is part of the learning process. In fact, the routines and practices Mrs. Jameson uses involve her encouraging students to value their willingness to explore an error for the efforts that led to it and the opportunities it provides to gain deeper understanding. Before each class, for example, Mrs. Jameson prepares different problem sets for small groups to solve. As they work on these together, she expects to hear them working out errors, theorizing, and problem solving together. When they get stuck, she acts as a coach, offering supportive suggestions. These activities are intended to empower all of her students to reflect on what they are learning and to see themselves as confident and capable mathematic analysts.

Here are some practical ways to foster a mistake-safe culture:

- Stress the value of effort and celebrate effort made.
- Frame errors with interest and curiosity, as a new starting point for learning instead of a dead end or a failed outcome.
- Encourage individual and collective error analysis and promote a culture of supportive feedback for problem solving.

Infusing Reflection Practices into Classroom Life

It's helpful to think of the type of reflection activities that we are advocating as the teacher acting as a coach and encouraging students to draw from their inner strengths. This type of coaching complements the findings of Stanford psychologist and researcher Carol Dweck (2006). Dweck found that students succeed more when we teach them to embrace the challenges and setbacks that come from their efforts to learn, show them the value of persistence, help them see that we value effort, and encourage and inspire them to do more. There are many ways that we can adopt this asset-based model, using what Dweck refers to as a *growth mindset*.

The Teachers College Reading and Writing Project model (Calkins, Kloss, & Vanderburg, 2018) is particularly helpful in bringing a growth mindset to language arts instruction. By putting teachers in the role of coach, this model encourages students to practice new skills purposefully on their own, but with the teacher standing by to offer guidance when needed. It promotes autonomy and empowerment by giving students experience in less structured small-group tasks and provides opportunities for one-to-one conferences with teachers and peers. Both Dweck's (2006) growth mindset philosophy and the workshop model of Calkins and colleagues (2018) are similar in philosophy and method to those embraced by many sports coaches and choral and musical directors: provide routine and continuous feedback and suggestions to expand participants' repertoire of expertise.

Like music and sports coaches, effective teachers of academic content supportively assign tasks for individuals and groups to practice in order to master new skills one at a time. They also provide consistent encouragement, motivation, and inspiration. They believe in and root for their learners. They closely monitor what individuals and groups do, provide specific and precise feedback about the positives they observe, and discuss strategies for making improvements. Then they repeat the same process to help everyone make efforts toward ongoing improvement, inviting reflection with questions such as these: *Do you think this makes it better? What else might you try?* This is the type of mindset that we advocate to create a mistake-safe classroom culture—one that explores and celebrates the journey of learning rather than the immediate results of an examination.

Some teachers tell us that immersion in this reflective, mistake-safe culture is like engaging a trusted friend to tell you what they see. You seek a friend's guidance because you believe you will get constructive, sympathetic, and accurate feedback that has your best interests in mind. The type of feedback that friends give is usually peppered with expressions of their care for and about you. They also ask questions about your experience, nudging you to think about what you learned and how you might apply it going forward. This is a model of learning designed to help the individual see and reflect on strengths and on possibilities: *What skills and talents do I have? What else could I do with my skills and talents?*

A general principle of responding effectively to students is to express appreciation of constructive behaviors (e.g., acknowledge students' deeds rather than their personal qualities). An example would be "That was a good bit of work you did making that map. The details are all there!" An example of a less desirable alternative is "You are always such a careful person!" Though the latter is a positive response, it deemphasizes the choices the student made and emphasizes things the student has less control over (e.g., personality, which many students view as fixed).

In addition, we encourage and empower students when our language avoids evaluative words like *never, always,* and *have to,* which feel like permanent judgments, and instead incorporates provisional comments, like *this time, maybe it would be better if,* and *you can decide if.* For example, if a student has had difficulty remembering to bring a homework folder to school, it can be undermining to say, "You have to remember to bring that homework folder back" (implying that you doubt his ability to do that). Responsive classroom expert Paula Denton (2007) argues for using positive alternative statements that underscore students' power to choose responsible action. For example, we might ask the same student, "What would be most helpful for you to remember to bring your homework folder to school tomorrow?"

Teachers can support students' self-reflection by encouraging them to listen to others, have empathy for others, express their feelings, and express their academic and social-emotional growth (Zacarian et al., 2017). Taking time to confer with individual students can help them see themselves as confident, capable learners and set goals and see possibilities for future growth. This can be especially powerful when we use a variety of supportive, encouraging, and positively focused self-assessment practices that are targeted for empowering students' self-advocacy as leaders of their own learning (Berger, Rugen, & Woodfin, 2014).

 Take a Closer Look: The Role of Self-Assessment and Reflection

An example of self-assessment and reflection comes from the Kansas City Schools partnership with the Truman Medical Center on trauma-sensitive school practices (Zacarian et al., 2017). The two partners co-developed a curriculum to help students respond to stressors more positively. One exercise involved providing elementary students prepared handouts with a writing prompt and space for a response. Learners drew pictures of their responses in the appropriate spaces. Under their drawings, they used their emerging writing skills to express their thoughts. One student drew a picture that depicted her answer to the writing prompt, *When I feel angry, I can. . . .* It was a figure in motion. Underneath the picture she wrote, "I can walk away."

Self-Assessment Practices That Build Self-Reflection Skills

Earlier in the chapter we saw how Mrs. Jameson, a mathematics teacher, encourages students to make mistakes and work collaboratively to find solutions by exploring the errors they make as they learn. As in the example shared, she regularly models her thinking aloud and makes mistakes to elicit her students' help in solving problem sets.

While teachers should encourage students to work in groups in a safe and positive manner, as Mrs. Jameson does, it's also important to engage students in self-assessment that will build self-reflection tools they will need in school and throughout their lives. There are many conventions for engaging students in reflection-focused self-assessment. We want to focus on three categories in particular: journal writing, teacher–student conferences, and student-led conferences.

Journal Writing

Journal writing is one of the most powerful tools for focusing students on their own academic and social-emotional learning and development. According to educational scholar Linda Suskie (2018), journal writing can strengthen students' thinking skills, including conceptual thinking, informational, metacognition, and synthesizing skills. In addition, student journal writing is an important vehicle for students' social-emotional growth (Durlak, Weissberg, Dymnicki, Taylor, & Schellinger, 2011; Konichi & Park, 2018).

There are many types of journal-writing tasks and activities that serve this purpose. According to Konichi and Park (2018), the common thread among all of them is that they are part of a sustained interactive conversation between teachers and students over time. Each journal-writing task should ask students to reflect on certain aspects of their learning and should do so in a productive and affirmative way that encourages students to focus on the positive takeaways of the experiences shared. This is most easily accomplished by providing specific writing prompts. We'll look at some prompt guidelines and examples shortly, but first, we want to highlight two formats for journal-writing exchanges.

Formats to Consider

Primarily, journal interactions between students and teachers are either written by hand and physically passed back and forth, like the math journals Robin Kendrick exchanges with her 4th grade students, or computer mediated. The latter allows for exchanges during class as well as asynchronously or synchronously outside class.

An example of computer-mediated communication comes from high school teacher Dave Gutierrez, who uses Google Docs to interact with students. Typically, he posts a question or task for each student to respond to by a certain date. Students use their computers to add their responses to the shared document during class or after school. If they post their response when Dave is online, he may interact with them in real time; otherwise, their responses are entered and saved by the due date, and Dave retrieves the various entries and responds to each. He has found this type of interactive exchange and repository to be enormously helpful. Students can share challenges that they are experiencing, seek solutions to strengthen their academic and social-emotional learning, and, most important, see a record of their personal growth.

Some additional benefits of computer-mediated journal exchanges between teachers and students are that they provide the potential for a more immediate response to student work than is possible with a traditional collect-comment-return arrangement, and they allow students to collaborate on the same document more easily. Students and teachers can share information readily and build connections with one another's personal, social, cultural, academic, and life experiences. In these ways, the practice can support and extend both academic and social-emotional learning.

Guidelines for Journal Response

Whether we use handwritten or computer-mediated journal exchanges with students, it is important to consider the ways in which we

- Honor students' efforts (including their mistakes) in a positive way.
- Are culturally responsive to the various identities of our students by encouraging, validating, and acknowledging their personal connections and competencies.
- Inspire and encourage them to do more.

Suggested Journal-Writing Prompts

The following are just four of the many journal prompts you might use to get started.

Summary entry. Ask students to write a summary of what they did to learn or achieve something. Let's say a group of young learners is engaging in a lesson on identifying their feelings in challenging situations, such as when they're afraid to do something. For this journal entry, students might respond to this prompt: *Discuss a time you did something even though you were afraid to do it*. You might expand the prompt by asking students to review the process by which they engaged in the challenging activity. Summary entry journal writing is an opportunity for students to think about their social and emotional strengths and how successfully completing a challenge was empowering to them.

Explanatory entry. Ask students to explain their thinking about the key ideas they explored or the key learning goals they have acquired. For example, high school biology students might explain the key differences between mitosis and meiosis. Another example comes from 4th grade teacher Robin Kendrick, who engages students in this type of self-assessment and reflection for each subject they study. In their math journals, students document their understandings of what they are studying and include any products that they create—such as comparison charts and original games. At regular intervals throughout the year, Robin meets with individual students to review how much they have learned. She feels that this is an especially powerful way for her to interact with reluctant learners who do not yet see themselves as confident in a particular subject.

Application entry. Ask students for a brief summary of the key takeaways from a unit of study that they will use in the future. An example comes from middle school social studies teacher James Newell. He asks students to respond to this prompt: *Discuss the key reasons why the Aztec religion changed when the Spanish arrived and how changes such as these affect societies.*

Reflection entry. Ask students to reconsider an experience, the events leading up to it, and/or their thoughts and feelings about what they learned from it. For example, a high school history teacher might regularly ask students to reflect on their perspective about a particular event that they are studying, periodically checking in to see if they have changed their perspective as they explore the event more deeply through the unit of study.

 Time for Reflection

Come up with two or three additional journal-writing prompts, including a rationale for each and an example of what it would look like in practice.

Teacher–Student Conferences

An additional method for engaging students in self-reflection is meeting with them on an individual basis. Across the K–12 spectrum, taking time to conference with students can be a powerful way to support them in feeling safe, acknowledged, competent, and empowered as learners and productive members of their classroom and school communities. A face-to-face conference can also be ideal for encouraging students to reflect on their accomplishments, successes, and challenges and set goals to be met over a designated amount of time (e.g., a week, a month, a semester). These conferences work best when they are collaborative and positively focused. Generally, they can occur during class time when the rest of the class is engaged in independent work, and they can be as short as 10 minutes.

It is helpful to maintain a standard set of routines and practices for teacher–student conferences so that these events are visible and known to everyone (see Figure 5.1).

FIGURE 5.1

Teacher–Student Conferences: Cycle of Routines and Practices

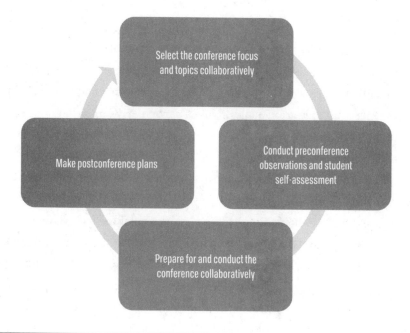

Let's take a closer look at each component in the cycle.

Select the conference focus and topics collaboratively. Just as it is important to have a pattern of routines and practices in our lessons so that students know what to expect, it is important to work collaboratively with students to select a conference focus and determine what will occur during and after the conference. This means there will be no surprises, which will help students feel in control and empowered. An example of a conference topic is sharing thoughts about what is going well in a particular area.

Just as in journal writing, question prompts can be useful in student–teacher conferences. The following are some prompts for engaging students (this is by no means a complete list; it is simply intended to help you get started in having conferences with students):

- What do you think is going well (e.g., in a specific subject, in pair or group discussions, in reading, writing, speaking, or listening)?
- When do you feel smartest (e.g., in a particular subject)?
- What is a challenge you are experiencing? What have you found to be the best way for addressing it?

Conduct preconference observations and student self-assessment. It's important to observe individual students before the conference in order to provide specific, positive feedback about what you have observed. Doing this supports students in seeing what they are capable of doing, particularly when they are persistent, when you encourage their efforts, and when you inspire them to do more and to be empowered using a growth mindset.

Prepare for and conduct the conference. It's also important to take time to plan for a student conference collaboratively. A helpful way to do this is to meet with the whole class to share thoughts and ideas for a particular conference topic and your purpose in making sure that it is focused on what is going well in a particular area. Examples of this type of planning might be to discuss holding an individual conference where students can preselect a piece of work that represents their best efforts and use the individual conferences for them to share specifically why it represents their best efforts and demonstrates their growth. Students might also opt to use the conference time to discuss challenges that they are experiencing in a particular area and plan to address the ways in which they think they need support. Even though the level of content may vary widely, the essential dynamic of supported reflection that leads to self-knowledge, confidence, and growth is the same with 1st graders as is it with high school students.

Make postconference plans. It is very helpful to conclude the conference on a positive, inspirational note that encourages the student in a specific way going forward. Indeed, this is a critical time to focus on what the student is doing well and plan for the next conference. You could make suggestions about next steps, describe what taking those steps will look like in a positive way, and, of course, encourage students in specific ways about what they are doing to be successful academically and social-emotionally.

Student-Led Conferences

Student-led conferences can be invaluable opportunities for students to share their learning with their teacher and families and, more important, be empowered to lead an event to share their accomplishments. According to Berger and colleagues (2014), these types of events help students organize their thoughts about their learning so they may communicate it to others, take responsibility for their learning, and strengthen a school's partnership with families, which we discuss in greater detail in Chapter 8. Just as teachers must organize the routines and practices that we use to teach and engage students in journal-writing exchanges and conferences with us, we must help students organize the student-led conference they will hold. Some schools may wish to forgo the traditional parent–teacher conference in favor of student-led conferences. This can be a very positive move for engaging students and their families throughout the year. However, it does not mean that we have any less of a role as educators. Rather, it requires that we collaborate closely with students, their families, faculty, and administrators to ensure that it is a worthwhile and positive experience.

To help ensure successful conferences, teachers should collaborate with students, colleagues, school leaders, families, and community partners to determine the following:

- *The design of student-led conferences*. When designed well, these meetings can be especially helpful in determining developmentally appropriate ways of engaging K–12 students. (We cover this in more detail in later chapters.)
- *The conference schedule*. Consider the time of year, day of week, and time of day that are likely to yield the greatest parent/guardian participation. For example, you may want to hold conferences directly before and after school as well as in the evening.
- *The student work that will be presented*. One method for engaging students in these events is to have them share a portfolio of their learning accomplishments. Students could share what they have learned by displaying it

creatively in a poster and explaining the steps they took to acquire specific knowledge.

- *The conference duration and agenda.* Berger and colleagues (2014) suggest that the conference last 20 to 40 minutes. We suggest allowing even more time when there are translators involved to ensure there is ample opportunity for two-way conversation.
- *The conference participants.* Students' primary caretakers could be two parents, a single parent, foster parents, grandparents, and strong extra-familial guardians. It is important that student-led conferences be inclusive of the full range of adults in students' lives who support their growth.
- *The means of encouraging family participation.* In many schools, there are the usual parents/guardians who come to every event and those who rarely attend an event. It's important to work closely with students, alumni within families, other parents and guardians, and school and community partners to support and encourage every family in attending.
- *How to respond to family input.* Plan and prepare for the type of questions that parents/guardians are likely to ask so that the conference is a positive and welcoming experience for all. (We cover this in more detail in later chapters.)
- *The follow-up actions.* Determine whether and when to have a follow-up meeting with students and colleagues to celebrate the student-led conference experience and discuss possible enhancements for future conferences.

* * * * *

In the next chapter, we discuss developing collaborative communication and conflict resolution skills, promoting respectful and fruitful academic discussion, seeing difference as opportunity, and setting goals to support an interdependent, collaborative culture of learning. We also provide strategies for using classroom-based extensions that enrich the development of this skill set by giving students the opportunity to experience real-world application.

The Skills of Collaboration

In Michael's class, students recognized that frequent small conflicts were creating a negative tone. At a classroom meeting, the students identified this problem and brainstormed a number of possible solutions. The proposal that garnered universal support was to create a chain made of colored strips of paper on which a classmate would acknowledge a specific good deed that someone else in the class had done on behalf of others.

Everyone liked this idea, but in order to implement it, they would first have to meet several challenges. What materials would they need beyond construction paper? Where would these materials be stored in the classroom? Would someone getting up to add a link to the chain of good deeds be disruptive? How could this project be managed without a teacher having sole responsibility for making it happen?

Here's what Michael's students did. Several volunteers stepped forward to form a "design team" that would cut strips of construction paper and maintain a supply of markers, tape, and staplers. They even made a precut paper-strip holder to keep the material organized. The design team also worked with classmates and their teacher to negotiate an agreed-upon location for the chain. Another group of student volunteers took a proprietary interest in promoting the project and encouraged classmates to participate when they arrived in the morning or at the end of the school day.

With a great deal of enthusiasm, yet another group of students made sure that the strips of good deeds were securely fastened into loops and that the chain was steadily extended along the wall.

As the good deeds accumulated, the chain grew longer, eventually extending along an entire wall of the classroom. Seeing this progress created a sense of pride that kept the students motivated to attend to the project. In the end, this deliberate focus on positive deeds generated a wave of constructive community building that had a positive ripple effect on the social-emotional tone of the classroom. Additionally, students demonstrated that they could execute a complex collaborative project under their own initiative, cooperating and solving problems along the way.

In this chapter, we explore how to empower student collaboration and look closely at the following topics, for the following reasons:

- **The central importance of communication.** Listening, self-expression, and conflict resolution are the foundation for harmonious and productive collaboration, and we emphasize the value of encouraging students to seek support and perspectives from the people in their lives.
- **The language and skills of cooperation.** The former is important because the words we use to communicate have a profound influence on learning and identity, and the latter matter because we cannot expect students to become more skilled in cooperation unless we actually teach those skills.
- **How to help students embrace the complexities of group work**. We look at both the process and task elements of group work, which is a powerful means of developing the skills of interdependence and collective autonomy.

Communication as the Lynchpin of Collaboration

Educators use a variety of terms to describe classroom collaboration, including *pairs and small groups, group work, group investigation, collaborative learning, cooperative learning, teamwork,* and *teams*. Chances are you have used some of these terms interchangeably. The type of collaboration that we're focusing on—the type that we believe fuels student empowerment—is summed up by Sharan (1990) as a classroom community effort in which no fewer than two and no more than six students are grouped to "work together to complete a group goal, share ideas, and help each other with answers to questions, share materials, and divide labor where appropriate" (p. 2). It's work that requires cooperation, listening, honest expression of ideas and feelings, respect for the contributions of others, and personal responsibility.

Many educational scholars claim that group work is a more successful method of teaching than the traditional lecture approach because it requires students to be highly active, interactive, and interdependent (Cohen & Lotan, 2014; Johnson & Johnson, 2009; Johnson, Johnson, & Holubec, 2008; Sharan, 1990). However, despite it being a proven instructional method, with various methodologies widely available, there is no guarantee that the collaborative activities teachers design will result in effective collaboration. In fact, you can probably summon to mind any number of examples of activities you've tried or witnessed that have fallen flat. At times, even the most seasoned educators have had occasion to wonder if having students work in groups is worth the effort. Our resounding response is always *yes, and* . . . . Yes, it's worth the effort, *and* it's up to educators to ensure that students have the supports they need to succeed. Among the most useful of these is communication support. Groups can't work well if group members don't listen to one another, don't share with one another, and don't know how to resolve conflicts if they arise.

For example, the "good deed" activity in Michael's classroom that we touted as a successful collaboration almost wasn't. It got off the ground quite well, and a few weeks in, there were a number of links in the chain. But Michael pushed for more. He took some time to check in with his students, asking them to reflect on how the project was going. It turned out that the students who were managing the craft supply table had a lot to share. They were sad and disappointed that the class's participation had fallen off from the initial enthusiasm. They assumed that their classmates had lost interest in doing it; with Michael's prompting, they said so publicly. Other students in the class were surprised. They stated with sincerity that they had simply forgotten to go to the table. Once this understanding was established, the table managers asked if it would be helpful to post a reminder sign, and the rest of the students agreed to this idea. This reflection activity, marked by honest communication, sparked a resurgence of participation in the project. In addition, it reinforced the value of listening and working together to come up with an effective solution where everyone felt empowered.

Helping Students Express Themselves . . . and Reserve Judgment

One way to foster the communication that's key to effective collaboration is to encourage students to name their feelings and take ownership of their thoughts without condemning one another. Psychologist Thomas Gordon (2016) calls this using the *language of acceptance*. In practice, it's the collective agreement that

- Each of us has the right to express our ideas and feelings.
- Each of us is to be respected as a person with ideas and feelings.
- Each of us can learn from other members of our group.

Just posting these agreements in a highly visible spot and referring to them regularly can make an impact.

It's also very helpful for educators to stay neutral in response to students' emotional experiences so that we can support them as they identify and talk through their feelings (as opposed to respond or react to our feelings about them). As an example, here is an interaction a student, Jackson, had with his middle school science teacher.

Jackson: I don't like it when Noah makes fun of me.

Teacher: I see.

Jackson: He stands right near me and makes fun of me in front of everyone.

Teacher: [Observing Jackson patiently, with curiosity and a sense of concern and understanding] Mmm-hmm.

Jackson: Well, maybe he didn't do it to be mean, but it bugs me.

 ## Time for Reflection

1. Imagine that you are Jackson's teacher. What neutral response might you give to his last statement to continue to support him in identifying and talking through his feelings?

2. Think of a recent incident when a student or a young person in your life came to you with a problem. What can you recall about your attitude or reactions as you listened? What do you think might have happened if you had said no words, or simply summarized your understanding of what you heard, back to them?

Helping Students Learn to Resolve Conflicts Themselves

Conflicts arise even in happy and harmonious classrooms. Our professional assumptions about emotional and physical safety do not necessarily mean that we can simply impose solutions, even peaceful ones, and expect students and families to automatically go along. Indeed, we can place students into collaborative groups or partnerships and group them with or away from students we believe they will or will not work constructively with. We can try to keep students from hurting each other physically and emotionally, and we can lead them to the doorway of conflict resolution, but it is ultimately their choice to go through it to share their truth and listen with empathy—whether their conflicts take the form of mild disagreements or impulsive rages.

Rather than view conflict and the expression of angry and sad feelings in school as things to be avoided at all costs, it can be helpful to think of them as productive opportunities that may allow students to learn how to become less reactive and less likely to inappropriately project their inner fears and insecurities onto others or magnify their reactions to small events. Overcoming disagreement may ultimately help them work more collaboratively. Over time, identification and acknowledgment of feelings creates the possibility that students can be authentically comfortable with their emotions and can trust themselves. The other end of the spectrum is when there is an illusion of peace through the absence of conflict. This occurs when educators banish inconvenient feelings from school. But emotions that are suppressed from being expressed or are banned altogether do not disappear. They are merely driven underground, and if they are negative, they resurface as petty conflicts, resistance to learning, student disempowerment, and hostility to oneself and others. Let's look at two easy strategies for instilling the habits of productive self-expression and conflict resolution.

Encourage "I" statements. According to Gordon (2000), encouraging students to use "I" statements express their emotions is a good practice. The first example in the pair below shows a language frame that students might use to help them express feelings that might otherwise lead to conflict. The second offers the possibility of resolving conflict by peacefully negotiating a mutually agreed-upon solution with a peer:

1. "When my learning is interrupted, I feel _____ because I have a need for _____."
2. "Would you be willing to _____?"

Use written agreements. Responsive classroom expert Ruth Charney (2002) suggests using guided written agreements to help students engage in resolution with others. As with any tool used to support students' development, it is helpful to provide students with models of such an agreement and guided practice in using it authentically. Figure 6.1 shows an example of an apology agreement.

FIGURE 6.1

Apology of Action Agreement

Apology of Action

I am sorry we had a problem between us. Sometimes just saying sorry is not enough. To make peace for our classmates, for each other, and for ourselves, I am willing to do something extra to help start the work of fixing it.

Because I recognize your need for

_____,

here is what I propose to do:

_____

_____

Sincerely,

_____

Time for Reflection

1. Imagine that you are Jackson and Noah's teacher. Describe how you would use tools like those described above to help students resolve a conflict.
2. In what ways would these actions support an overall goal of collaboration and teamwork?

Instructional coach Jennifer Hunter, whom we quoted in Chapter 2, explains how she uses conflict resolution techniques to support student empowerment.

 Take a Closer Look: Conflict Resolution

I like to remind students to use active listening skills and specific language frames to help them resolve a conflict. One specific example of this was when I was facilitating a STEM activity with a 4th grade language-based classroom. The students were asked to build a device that would hold an apple on the top of their heads while they ran a relay race. The 4th graders were put into groups of three or four students. During the 30 minutes of time they had to build, I noticed one boy was not participating in the group that he was assigned to. He explained to me that he was upset because he had a different idea and his teammates were not listening to him.

I asked that his teammates stop and hear what he had to say. First, I had him explain how he was feeling using a "I feel ___ when I ___" construction. Providing students time to communicate with each other and explain how they felt about the situation allowed them to resolve the problem on their own. I usually try to avoid offering a solution to the problem, especially with older students. In this situation, I did not have to intervene at all, and the group of students decided to incorporate one idea that everyone had to build the device. At the end of the relay, I went back to that group of students and told them that I was really proud of the way they had worked together to solve the problem so that all members of the group were able to participate. I believe that teaching students to use conflict resolution strategies to solve their problems on their own is empowering.

—Jennifer Hunter, instructional coach, Brockton, Massachusetts

Gathering Support for Student-Led Conflict Resolution

A wholehearted embrace of student-led conflict resolution is a powerfully visionary goal, but it's easier said than done. Honestly, you need all the support you can get, which is why we advise enlisting the help of other students, families, colleagues, school leaders, and community members. These partners can be especially valuable when initial efforts to resolve conflicts are ineffective. Here is an example.

Scott, a 2nd grader, was not aggressive by nature, but when he went after his classmate, Alan, in the coatroom after school, he insisted he had a good reason for doing so. He claimed that earlier in the day, Alan (who was boisterous and silly—and fond of getting reactions out of people) had been mean to him. Scott explained that when Alan got too close in the coatroom and actually bumped into him, he couldn't help but react. Just as Scott was about to hit Alan, the teacher swooped in to separate the boys.

If this conflict had taken place earlier in the day, the teacher would have given Scott and Alan a moment to cool down and then led them in a conversation designed to work out their differences. Because it was dismissal time and the boys had buses to catch, this conversation was postponed until the next day. However, both boys came in that morning quite reluctant to resolve their conflict. Scott explained that his grandfather had told him, "If anyone lays a hand on you, you hit them right back in the stomach—hard!" Alan had received similar advice from his family: fight back or risk becoming a victim, possibly for a lifetime.

The relationship between these classmates was ultimately repaired by a supported conference informed by input from both families. During the conference, Alan and Scott had a chance to be heard, and they were led to empathize with each other and identify the feelings and underlying needs that the other had experienced in the conflict. The process was based on the principles of nonviolent communication. After acknowledging to each other that their grievance had been heard and their frustrations with each other had been released—or at least made tolerable—they voluntarily agreed to perform an act of kindness (with teacher encouragement): creating and delivering a holiday card for the school secretary. That act of kindness allowed them to restore their feeling of membership in a community and put their conflict behind them. All of this occurred because of the teacher's commitment to understanding points of view—gathered from conversations with the students' families—that were different from his own. By talking with and listening to Scott, Alan, and their families, he gained insights into each boy's motivations and was able to come up with a positive, strengths-based response to their conflict.

When helping students work together and resolve conflict, it is advantageous to seek help from others to put together a reflective, responsive, and empathetic approach that takes into account a broad range of perspectives and approaches. Reaching out to colleagues, students' families, and others can provide fresh perspectives. Let's look back at Scott and Alan's conflict. When the two students reported their reluctance to resolve their differences, let alone their conflict, and shared what their parents and grandparents had advised, their teacher asked if it would be OK to speak with their families. They both readily agreed. When Scott's father met with the teacher, he told him about his experience as a young child emigrating from Cape Verde to Massachusetts in the 1990s. He and his younger brother had been singled out because of their racial identity and threatened on the school bus, and this bullying went on for years. Scott's teacher listened with an open heart to the father's painful experience and readily acknowledged the need to protect Scott from undergoing something similar. He then met with Alan's mother and learned that, as a child, she had been bullied about her weight. Alan's mother talked about the names she had been called and how much she wanted Alan to be spared that kind of treatment. Empathetically listening to these experiences helped the boys' teacher understand the advice the parents had given their children. It also helped him be open to their candor and led to a productive discussion of potential resolutions to the boys' conflict.

The next day, after the two parent meetings, Scott and Alan's teacher was able to listen to each student separately without judgment and hear about the feelings that had led to their conflict. Rather than pronounce Scott's physical aggression wrong or restate a rule as though it were a solution (e.g., "Shoving is not how we resolve problems at our school"), the teacher communicated that he understood each boy's feelings and that he cared about them. He stressed that he wasn't drawing a permanent or negative conclusion about Scott.

When conflict arises in a classroom, educators have to think very carefully about the factors that diversity of any kind (racial, ethnic, linguistic, cultural, learning differences, physical challenges, gender, sexual orientation, etc.) has on any student and how that affects them and their families. We also have to consider the types of solutions that will be feasible and mutually agreeable in a particular situation *and* ensure students have a voice in the decision making. For these reasons, gathering the support of others is invaluable.

As mentioned earlier, sociologists Steele and Aronson (1995) coined the term *stereotype threat* to describe the feeling of being in jeopardy as a result of a negative stereotype. In our example, Scott felt that he was being threatened by a peer. And he was told by his family that he should feel at risk because of his racial identity and to fight back with any means possible if he felt he was being hurt. While we can empathetically understand the effect that discriminatory experiences had on his parents, this is not the same as experiencing this discrimination ourselves.

Stereotype threat is pervasive and incendiary in our schools, and research confirms this (Cohen & Lotan, 2014; Steele, 2010; Steele & Aronson, 1995). Educators cannot ignore it. However, it is also true that we often react to students' conflicts (e.g., from when they politely disagree to when they physically fight) based on our own perceived status about ourselves and/or our students, which affects how we learn together and collaborate. Our own unexamined norms may prevent us from considering our students' and their families' ways of being and acting as legitimate and reasonable.

It can be challenging to problem solve with students and families and come up with a "just right" solution. What is effective and appropriate for communicating with one set of parents or guardians may not be for another. Our job is to find common ground in what matters most to them, based on what we have heard them say, and then make accurate emotional inferences from their tone of voice and body language. In addition, the experiences that shape their values and priorities may make certain priorities more prominent. It's imperative that we recognize what those priorities are and address them by seeking the support of others, engaging in professional development to further our understanding, and giving students opportunities to work and socialize together. In the case of Scott and Alan, their parents' experiences of powerlessness in their own childhoods led them to prioritize the development of the boys' self-defense skills over their practice of conflict resolution.

Figure 6.2 summarizes some common unspoken assumptions parents and guardians may have that, when left unaddressed, can be obstacles to students resolving their problems autonomously in school and working collaboratively with others.

FIGURE 6.2

Addressing Common Family Beliefs and Concerns

If it looks like they believe . . .	Assure them that . . .
Society is competitive and they want their child to have every advantage.	You can be an ally in helping their child get ahead.
Their child is sensitive and likely to be taken advantage of by others.	You are vigilant on their child's behalf and will be a guide and protector.
Their child has been misunderstood.	You appreciate their child and are on their child's side.
Their child needs limits.	You will set firm limits.
Their child has a creative spirit that needs freedom and understanding.	You will provide freedom and understanding.
Their child has undeveloped potential.	You will offer challenge.
Their child lacks social skills.	You will be patient, and you will offer guidance.
Showing emotions is a sign of weakness.	You will encourage all students to identify and express the emotional effects of their and others' behavior.
It's important to solve problems by being a "tattletale."	You will encourage all students to draw on authority as a tool to ensure safety.
Someone who has wronged you deserves punishment.	You will encourage a restorative justice model.
They will not be listened to.	You will listen actively with an open mind to their account of events and concerns.

Applying These Lessons in Our Own Collaborative Efforts

We've stressed throughout this book the value of modeling for our students the skills we want them to master. The same holds when it comes to communicating in a way that supports effective collaboration. When working with others, it's important to

- Engage in open dialogue (without being judgmental) with students, families, colleagues, supervisors, and other stakeholders.
- Listen and be open-minded to what we hear and learn.
- Value and be interested in—and even curious about—others' opinions, thoughts, and ideas as well as their willingness to collaborate with us.
- Articulate and encourage belief in positive outcomes for our students.

Time for Reflection

How might you adapt Figure 6.2 when collaborating with colleagues on behalf of Alan and Scott's conflict resolution?

Scott and Alan's teacher fostered a condition in which there was an expectation of a positive outcome, unconditional acceptance, and interdependence in a community of trust. Operating from these conditions is essential. It allowed the teacher in this example to enact a plan that encouraged a productive, positive outcome for everyone involved.

After the teacher met with the parents and both of the students, Scott and Alan agreed to sign apology agreements. Scott's said that he understood Alan's need for safety. He promised that the next time a conflict arose between them, he would use words instead of physical actions. He also offered to clean Alan's locker. Alan acknowledged Scott's apology and his need for respect and offered to help him with homework if Scott wanted that. Finally, they teamed up to do an act of kindness for the school secretary, whom they both liked very much. Thus, their agreements were a collaborative reflection of what they, their teacher, and their families reasoned would be most successful. In addition, these agreements reflected their teacher's capacity to listen to the students and their parents; have empathy for them; attend to their values, assets, and strengths; mediate their emotions; and resolve conflict in a productive, positive way.

 Time for Reflection

1. Imagine you are speaking with a parent or colleague whose values or attitudes about homework, discipline, or conflict resolution are very different from yours. What are three to four strategies you might use to help them know they are being heard?
2. Describe a time when listening without offering your opinion or advice helped you better understand a student or parent or colleague. What did you learn?
3. If what you learned proved constructive, in what ways did this information support a deepening of your relationship or ability to solve a problem?

Promoting the Language and Skills of Cooperation

Carefully chosen words and phrases can promote or discourage student voice and cooperation in our classrooms (Denton, 2007). Here are some guidelines, concepts, and phrases that are important to teach explicitly in order to create a constructive and empowering basis for cooperative learning work:

- In group discussions, students should use their classmates' names when discussing or referring to the contributions those classmates are making (e.g., "Taylor said that one of the causes of the Civil War was economic differences between the North and the South"). Using a name conveys respect for the person and his or her idea, and it ensures all ideas are credited appropriately.
- When disagreeing with a point in a discussion, students should acknowledge that point before offering their counterpoint (e.g., "I understand Arlo's perspective, but I see things differently"). From there, students can explain how their idea differs and what experience or information causes them to see it that way. Again, this practice shows respect for others' ideas and contextualizes the differences in perspective.
- When describing a struggle to succeed at something, students should say "I'm/we're working on that" rather than "I'm bad at that." This positive framing avoids stigmatizing the process of becoming.
- When making a request of another person, students should acknowledge that complying with it is a choice (e.g., "Would you be willing to read what I've written and give me your feedback?"). Doing so demonstrates respect for peers' sense of independence and sidesteps the risk of resistance to being commanded.
- When giving someone positive feedback on an action, students should look for ways to name specific aspects they have appreciated (e.g., "When I read your story, I learned so much about skateboarding that I didn't know!" rather than "What a great story!"). Specific appreciation establishes an emotional connection and suggests a path to continued learning.

Pre-Teaching and Re-Teaching the Skills of Cooperating

Pre-teaching and re-teaching skills is a powerful way to implement cooperative learning in the classroom. The following is a list of foundational skills that merit explicit attention, no matter what grade level you teach. Each might be the subject of a lesson or coaching meeting with students, individually or in groups:

- How to share work equitably so all group members participate
- How to listen to ideas openly without inhibiting others from taking risks
- How to politely guide others back on task
- How to take advantage of the strengths of a group or partnership
- How to set goals and manage time
- How to get help when stuck
- How to negotiate disagreement
- How to work respectfully with people who have a different communication or thinking style than you
- How to see differences as strengths
- How to reflect on a process to improve it as you go
- How to communicate support and commitment to your partner or teammates
- How to allow others to be right
- How to share the floor when you are speaking too much, or come forward when you are not speaking enough
- How to deal with an unexpected obstacle
- How to brainstorm for solutions before choosing one

Helping Students Embrace Group Work

Helping students understand the complexities of working together should be a top priority for us if we hope to support them in understanding other perspectives and developing the social-emotional language and dispositions they need in school and throughout their lives. In order to provide this support, we must be able to distinguish between the skills students need to have a voice and agency in the communicative process of group work and the skills they need to engage successfully in the academic learning task.

Consider the example of Taylor, a student in a high school U.S. history class. Her teacher tells the class to separate into small groups of four. Taylor watches her classmates form groups, hoping and waiting to be selected. She tries her best to make eye contact with the other students while quietly saying to herself, "Pick me, please pick me." After a few minutes, she realizes that her peers have almost entirely separated into groups and that she has not been chosen. As she is realizing this, a classmate asks her to join his group. As Taylor walks over to join that group, she worries that her classmate has only asked her to join because he feels sorry for her, that she won't be accepted by her peers, and that she will say something that the group might think is dumb. Throughout the group's interactions, Taylor remains silent, afraid to speak for fear that she will not be accepted by them.

An additional example is Stephan, who is in the same class as Taylor. Stephan doesn't like working in teams or groups; group work is too slow for him, there are too many issues between students, and he always feels like he is carrying the load of everyone because he's known as the "smart one." When Stephan's teacher announces a group project to research and create a presentation about the causes of World War I, Stephan deflates. He thinks to himself that he already knows the reasons for the war and cannot bear the thought of being in a group. At the same time, he knows that one of his teacher's grading criteria is "working with others" and that he will have to do that to get a good grade. As Stephan's group gathers, he begins by blurting out that he already knows the answers to the group's questions. He talks over his classmates and dominates their discussion. After five minutes, Stephan raises his hand and tells the teacher that the group has finished their discussion and would like paper to complete the task.

 ## Time for Reflection

Place a check mark in the boxes that most apply to Taylor and Stephan.

Student	Listens to others	Asks questions	Contributes to the group's process	Positively acknowledges others' comments and ideas
Taylor				
Stephan				

1. Based on the check marks you have made, describe how Taylor and Stephan do or do not engage in collaborative learning.
2. Look back at the definition of *group work*. How does your description of Taylor and Stephan define what collaborative learning is and is not?

The Process Element of Group Work

While the examples we have presented in this chapter (featuring Scott, Alan, Taylor, and Stephan) are quite distinct from one another, they exemplify a few of the many dynamic complexities of the communicative process involved in group work. By *communicative process,* we mean the ways in which students gather, work, and communicate together (Zacarian, 2013; Zacarian et al., 2017; Zacarian & Silverstone, 2015). It encompasses how students share their beliefs and ideas, deliberate, and come to agreement. In the examples of Taylor and Stephan, neither student engaged in the communicative process of collaboration. Taylor did not participate at all, and Stephan monopolized the group without taking time to listen to others, let alone to deliberate and come to agreement with them. In order to truly collaborate, all students need to be willing to share their ideas, listen attentively to others, engage in collaborative reflection, and agree on their group's process. It requires them to engage in social-emotional behaviors that help one another feel safe, a sense of belonging, acknowledged, and competent. In other words, we want students to see group work as full of positive possibilities, where everyone has something important and valuable to offer.

Fortunately, we can foster both these skills and attitudes. Children learn how to collaboratively communicate through repeated exposure to, observations of, and interactions with others. This occurs most successfully when we provide them with

- Repeated guided instruction about collaboration.
- Models of collaborative communication.
- Encouragement and support to engage in collaborative behaviors.

To develop a culture where successful partner and group work can occur, teachers can build a foundation of skills and experiences that encourage students to participate in their classroom community. It is useful to have a repertoire of activities that foster students' trust, communication, empathy, and ability to see others' perspectives. Here are some we recommend.

- *What's Alike and What's Different:* Partners take five minutes to try to find as many similarities and differences as they can, including number of siblings, interests, skills, and experiences. *Benefits:* Establishes commonality and respect for differences.

- *Talking and Listening:* Students are separated into groups of three (listener, speaker, and observer). One student tells a brief story on a designated subject, which is heard without comment by the listener. On completion of the story, the listener says back, as precisely as they can, what they heard. The observer offers confirmation or correction of the details. *Benefits:* Affirms individual points of view and experience and promotes close listening.

- *Compliments and Kindness:* The group brainstorms ways students might want to receive acts of kindness. Students' names are written on pieces of paper and placed in a container. Individually, volunteers withdraw a classmate's name from the container and agree to secretly do a good deed for the classmate during a designated amount of time (a day, a week, two weeks, etc.). *Benefits:* Fosters an atmosphere of warmth and cooperation in a class as students experience multiple small actions that support the idea of a kind and safe community.

- *Just Like Me:* A group leader reads a series of specific statements, such as "I like to sing," "I have a cat in my house," or "I find the algebra homework really hard." Students for whom the various statements are also true say, "Just like me!" The statements selected can spotlight characteristics or interests that otherwise might not come to light. *Benefits:* Provides a low-risk means for group members to get to know one another.

The Task Element of Group Work

An additional element of group work to consider is the collaborative academic task that we ask students to engage in. If the process element is *how* we want students to approach the work, the task element reflects *what we want them to do* and *how that will support their academic thinking and growth.* A key aspect of this is selecting (or co-selecting with students) tasks that fully engage them in a positive, productive way. According to Dweck, Walton, and Cohen (2014), the key for teachers is to "seek challenging tasks that are challenging for students to learn" (p. 4). It is also critical to select tasks that are most likely to captivate students' interests and sustain their investment in completing the task throughout their academic exploration.

Here are some examples of collaborative academic tasks from elementary, middle, and high school settings:

- *Elementary school:* First grade students are studying weather patterns in their science class. Each day for 10 days, students individually complete a chart depicting the weather (see Figure 6.3). The teacher asks students to work in pairs to compare their charts and respond to the following question: Which weather pattern has been most common for the past 10 days: sunny, windy, or rainy?
- *Middle school:* Students work together to determine the main causes of the U.S. Civil War in their social studies class based on information from their

FIGURE 6.3

1st Grade Students' Weather Chart

SUNDAY	MONDAY	TUESDAY	WEDNESDAY	THURSDAY	FRIDAY	SATURDAY
	1 ☀	2 ☀	3 ☀	4 ☀	5 ☀	6 🌬
7 🌬	8 🌧	9 🌧	10 🌧	11	12	13
14	15	16	14	18	19	20
21	22	23	24	25	26	27
28	29	30	31			

textbook and their in-class discussions. To engage in this task, they have been separated into small groups of four. Each student is tasked with presenting one or two causes for the Civil War and specifying where they found this information in the textbook or class notes. After hearing each group member's causes, as a group they come to agreement about what they think are the two most relevant causes of the Civil War.

- *High school:* Students are reading Act I, Scene 3 of *Romeo and Juliet* in their English language arts class. The teacher has separated the class into small groups and tasks them with using sock puppets to act out 20 key lines from this part of the play that highlight the themes they are exploring.

 Time for Reflection

Describe the differences between the process and task elements of group work.

The task element of group work design calls for educators to capture students' individual and collaborative interests in subject-matter learning so that they are compelled to learn. Let's look more closely at the high school English language arts example to demonstrate what we mean.

In this class, students are tackling the complex language of Shakespeare. For many students, this older form of English is quite challenging to understand. Rather than focus on the language as the key lever to understand the play, the teacher identifies an academic task that he thinks will be compelling for students: creating and acting out a sock puppet play of Act I, Scene 3. He separates students into five groups of four and asks them to work creatively to direct and act their own version of the scene by reducing it to 20 key lines. To get them started, he tells them that they will see three movie clips of the same scene; the first is in modern English, a language they are all familiar with, as they use it every day, and the second two are in Shakespeare's early modern English. He talks about the common themes from this scene: love versus hate and fate versus choice. He then shows the three movie clips. Afterward, he guides the small groups in discussing the differences they observed between the movie clips. Drawing from their discussions, he then guides students in tackling their assignment. Using Google Docs, he shows the class how to reduce the scene to 20 lines. In the classroom, he puts one table on top of another and turns it on its side so that the top of the table is facing the class. Using a box of sock puppets, he hides behind the table to demonstrate how to enact the sock puppet show. Students then work collaboratively to reduce the scene to the 20 key lines that they believe depict the themes. Each student selects a character to play. During the last segment of class, each small group enacts their sock puppet play. Afterward, the teacher guides them in a discussion about the lines that each group chose and the creative direction that they took to enact the play. All of these supported activities lead students to become more empowered in their own learning and boost social and academic interactions in the process.

* * * * *

In the next chapter, we explore why it's so important for students to practice the skills of self-advocacy.

Self-Advocacy

In Chapter 1, we named Malala Yousafzai as an inspirational figure that teachers refer to when we ask them to cite the ultimate example of an empowered student. While Malala is a brave, influential, and thoroughly remarkable person, the type of self-advocacy that she exercised in stepping forward and speaking up for the rights of girls and women is a dramatic example of the very same skill we want all students to develop. Every student will face circumstances in which it is essential to advocate for their own ideas, needs, and desires as well as those of others, even in the face of risk and challenge. All acts of self-advocacy require the practice and development of the same fundamental skills. This is true whether we are looking at an introverted person asking a teacher to clarify a direction or the bold, activist student speakers from Parkland, Florida, engaging in public advocacy to change a national discussion.

Self-advocacy is something children will use throughout their development and in adulthood. In this chapter, we look closely at the development of self-advocacy capacity by exploring the following topics:

- **The definition of self-advocacy and its various forms.** A common understanding of the terminology helps clarify how we can support students' ability to self-advocate.

- **Opportunities for self-advocacy in the classroom.** It is important for students to identify and learn how to effectively express their ideas, their needs, and their desires.
- **Ways to help students advocate for themselves while also respecting others.** Balancing personal assertiveness with respect for others allows for both self-awareness and social adeptness.
- **Practical approaches to developing self-advocacy skills.** There are general principles and practices that support the development of self-advocacy in all students.

What Is Self-Advocacy?

The term *self-advocacy* is often used interchangeably with *self-empowerment* and *empowerment* by those who study sociology and education (e.g., Blankstein & Noguera, 2015; Noguera, 2015), social justice (e.g., Gorski & Pothini, 2018), students with disabilities (e.g., Roberts, Ju, & Zhang, 2014), students living with poverty (e.g., Budge & Parrett, 2018; Jensen, 2009), bilingual education (e.g., Baker, Wright, & Cook, 2017; Soltero, 2016), and collaborative learning (Cohen & Lotan, 2014). We have also heard the term *voice* used to reference an aspect of self-advocacy—that is, the assertion of preference, values, and beliefs in relation to a learning decision. When we use the term *self-advocacy* in this book, we are referring to three different types of communicative actions that students can take in order to better their immediate circumstances, better their lives in general, or better the lives of others. Students self-advocate when they identify and express their ideas, their needs, and their desires so that these can be illuminated, acknowledged, supported, validated, valued, and changed.

Let's look at some examples of the three types of self-advocacy.

Self-advocacy that expresses an idea. Second grade teacher Wanda Nieves is teaching a math unit that involves using timelines to calculate elapsed time. A student named Atif suggests a new classroom activity: working in teams to create a horizontal timeline to display the daily classroom schedule.

Self-advocacy that expresses a need. Mrs. Nieves is reviewing her students' math work. Although Emma has solved a particularly challenging calendar problem, there's evidence that Emma has attempted to erase some large, desperate-looking scribbles underneath her solution. Before Mrs. Nieves can ask Emma about these, Emma walks up to her and says, "I don't really get this, Mrs. Nieves. How do you do it?"

Self-advocacy that expresses a desire. Mrs. Nieves is separating students into small groups to collaboratively solve problem sets. As usual, she assigns each a student a role within his or her group: the facilitator, who leads the group in completing its academic task; the ask-the-teacher person, who checks with the teacher when the group is unsure of a process; the notetaker, who acts as the group's scribe and documents their collaborative work; and the showcase person, who presents the group's solutions to the whole class. Olivia wants to be her group's showcase person. She expresses this wish to Mrs. Nieves, who smiles to signal her affirmative response and assigns Olivia this role.

It's exciting when a student who hasn't previously spoken up comes forward and shares an idea, expresses the need for support or clarification, or expresses a desire. Of course, we want all of our students to actively and honestly communicate with us. It is an invaluable and constructive element of our work with them (even as, and especially when, it may seem to complicate things in the short run). The students in our examples from Mrs. Nieves's class do just that.

Here are a few more examples of advocating for oneself to express a need:

- A student cannot see the front of the classroom because of a physical barrier and shares this issue with his teacher.
- A student tells the teacher that she's having trouble reading the "fuzzy" or "blurry" words on the board.
- A student cannot hear clearly because of distracting noises or a hearing impairment and lets his teacher know.
- A student identifies hunger, the need for shelter or medical care, or a distracting physical sensation or social-emotional barrier as an obstacle to her ability to learn or participate in class comfortably.

These are just some of the infinite possible scenarios of student self-advocacy. Though they are often a response to a practical personal need, they might also be motivated by visionary or altruistic motives: the desire to volunteer, lead, or participate in an activity; the need to communicate an idea or a deeply held value; or the need to extend, strengthen, or affirm the ideas of others. It might begin with a practical personal need, but it can extend to the impulses that lead us to serve our community and even our world.

Time for Reflection

1. Write an additional example of self-advocacy in the form of articulating an idea.
2. Write an additional example of self-advocacy in the form of communicating a need.
3. Write an additional example of self-advocacy in the form of expressing a desire.

It is important to remember, though, that many students *do not* speak up on behalf of themselves or others. Let's look at three additional examples from Wanda Nieves's class.

- When Mrs. Nieves calls for volunteers to explain how they solved a word problem involving liquid measurement, Jackson thinks about raising his hand. But he immediately remembers Atif, who had just spoken out of turn to call out his answers and was redirected to wait for someone who raised their hand to speak first. Maybe volunteering an answer would upset Atif. So Jackson keeps his hand down and says nothing.
- Aiden sits in the back corner of the classroom next to the radiator. When the heat comes on, the radiator can be so loud that he has a hard time discerning what his teacher and classmates are saying. He is too nervous to tell anyone that he has trouble hearing when this happens because he is afraid that his friends and classmates will make fun of him. Saketh noticed the loud radiator noise the other day when he and Aiden were partnering on a task, but he's not sure if he should speak up for his classmate.
- Alexis loves being the facilitator in a small group. She often imagines what it would be like to be a teacher. When it's time for small-group activities, she always hopes that her teacher will assign her to this role. But unlike teachers

Alexis has had before, Mrs. Nieves only assigns the facilitator role to students who volunteer for it. Alexis doesn't feel brave enough to do that.

There are various reasons why students might not speak up—a lack of confidence in themselves; concern about their social status, abilities, differences, disabilities, and relationships; simple shyness; not having the English words to adequately express themselves; being a Black student in a majority-white class who doesn't want to rock the boat by speaking up against a microaggression . . . the list goes on and on. There are also many students who speak up but do so in ways that are not constructive; perhaps their comments promote classroom disharmony, disrupt or inhibit others' learning, or break the agreed-to norms of interaction. As such, self-advocacy can have a negative influence on a community. It is helpful for educators to distinguish negative or destructive behavior from self-advocacy and discourage the former without discouraging the latter. Consider three more examples from Wanda Nieves's class:

- Hala interrupts a classmate to shout out her own idea. When Mrs. Nieves asks her to wait her turn, Hala is impatient. "I already know the answer!" she says.
- During an explanation his teacher is giving, Anthony sighs loudly and says, "This is so boring. Are we having outdoor recess today, Mrs. Nieves?"
- As they begin a group task, Madelyn informs teammates Anthony and Hala that *she* should be the recorder since she is the smartest one in the group.

Opportunities to Build Self-Advocacy Skills

A school day presents a constant stream of situations, large and small, that demand self-advocacy skills. And that is great news for our students, because school is the ideal place to develop, practice, and strengthen these skills.

Classroom environments that promote empowerment do so by providing multiple opportunities for students to build their confidence and capacity to speak up, address issues, take risks, and actively participate in and contribute to what works. Teachers can and should actively look for and create opportunities for all students—even the ones who are typically less assertive or forthcoming—to engage in these acts of advocacy.

Here's another example to consider, offered by instructional coach Jennifer Hunter. Many of Jennifer's students are recently arrived in the United States, and she takes deliberate steps to provide them with voice and choice in their learning. For example, after hearing from her students that they like computer games and working on computers, she came up with an idea.

Take a Closer Look: Supporting Self-Advocacy Through Voice and Choice

Many of our students experienced trauma before or during their transition to the United States, and some are still experiencing it now.

I discovered that offering a traumatized child a choice can be very empowering because it gives them control over what they do or don't do. Here's an example. My students take the state-mandated test for English learners. One year, I was asked to administer it to a specific student who sometimes shut down when he became frustrated. Knowing this, I went into his classroom and spoke with him about his choices. I explained that I had some work for him to do on a tablet that I had. I showed him what it looked like and asked him if he would like to work with me today or tomorrow. He agreed to work with me that day, but as the questions became increasingly difficult, he did not want to continue. At times, his stamina to work through difficult questions was low.

I also knew that he was competitive and that he liked to race his friends at recess, so I asked him if he would like to race me. His eyes immediately lit up with excitement. I offered an idea: he would be able to challenge me to a race for each assessment that he completed. We had to complete four separate tests, one for each language domain (listening, speaking, reading, and writing). I was hoping that this would give him motivation to push through the frustration and work to his potential. Ultimately, he completed all of the testing sessions, and now we use "Racing Mrs. Hunter" as a monthly incentive to keep him motivated.

I have found that the strategy of offering a choice does not just work during testing. There are many occasions in school during which students may shut down—during math work, writing, reading comprehension activities, and so on. Overall, when I am able to provide a student with a choice, it usually benefits them and myself.

—Jennifer Hunter, instructional coach, Brockton, Massachusetts

Jennifer provides a fine example of how identifying what matters to our students and allowing them to exercise a meaningful choice can be empowering. Figure 7.1 presents additional examples of advocacy activities.

FIGURE 7.1

Opportunities for Advocacy in K–12 Classrooms

Grade Levels	Activities	Examples
K–2	Decide on a welcoming greeting.	Students determine the type of welcoming greeting that will occur when they gather in the morning (e.g., welcome song).
3–12	Collaboratively create the classroom design.	Students express ideas, needs, and desires for their classroom design (e.g., placement of learning stations, displays, desks, etc., for ease of learning and participating in small-group and pair learning).
K–12	Students express an idea—their own or someone else's.	Students use sticky notes to communicate ideas to the teacher without interrupting a lesson.
	Engage in a classroom council.	Classroom councils allow students to collaboratively propose, test, and modify solutions to problems, expressing their own desires or someone else's.

Balancing Self-Advocacy and Respect for Others

Students need to learn how to advocate for their own needs and values while respecting the needs and values of others. Teachers can support this by working to balance students' assertiveness and receptivity skills. Figure 7.2 provides descriptive examples of both.

FIGURE 7.2

Finding the Skill Balance for Effective Self-Advocacy

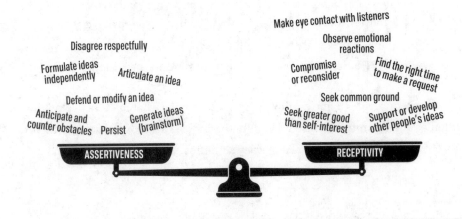

The specific skills that need to be developed or strengthened will vary from person to person, based on their life experiences and temperament. Take, for example, a shy 5th grader named Daniel, who rarely engages in self-advocacy behaviors (see Figure 7.3).

FIGURE 7.3

A Student with Emerging Self-Advocacy Skills (Pre-Assertive)

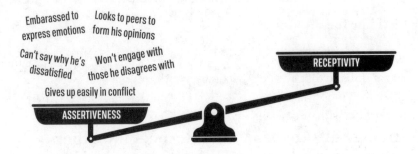

Daniel: A shy student who rarely engages in self-advocacy behaviors.

Now, in contrast, consider self-assured 5th grader Elsa, who is a strong but ineffective self-advocate (see Figure 7.4).

FIGURE 7.4

A Student with Emerging Self-Advocacy Skills (Pre-Receptive)

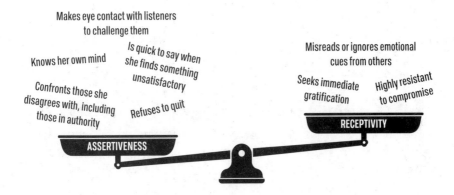

Elsa: An outspoken student who is an enthusiastic but ineffective self-advocate.

If we consider the personality differences among students in a classroom, we realize that the developmental paths they must take to self-advocacy inevitably differ. Some need to become more assertive in their ability to share their perspectives with others, while other may have to become observant and receptive to those around them. The ultimate destination, however, is the same: achieving just the right balance that simultaneously allows for both self-awareness and social adeptness.

 Time for Reflection

1. What are some classroom activities that would help Daniel strengthen his social skills so that he might become a better self-advocate?
2. What are some classroom activities that would help Elsa learn to be effective in working with others while meeting her own needs?

Developing Self-Advocacy Capacity

The human brain is quite malleable and has the capacity to build new pathways for thinking, acting, and reacting (Floyd & McKenna, 2003; Lerner et al., 2005). As such, we might think of self-advocacy as having various stages of development, from *pre-emerging*, where none is evidenced, to *emerging, developing, enacting,* and *integrating* (see Figure 7.5). Indeed, there are so many gradations along the spectrum of self-advocacy that it is important to have a framework for understanding what it is and how it is evidenced.

FIGURE 7.5

Continuum of Self-Advocacy Development

| Pre-Emerging | Emerging | Developing | Enacting | Integrating |

All students can benefit from practicing the social-emotional communication skills that are needed for learning, socializing, and working collaboratively. While we might see ourselves as primarily instructors of a particular discipline or subject, we also are the primary instructors in guiding students to develop social-emotional communication skills like listening; empathy; emotional regulation; the ability to recognize their own values, assets, and strengths (and those of others); and the ability to resolve conflicts (Zacarian et al., 2017).

Children must be provided with multiple and sustained opportunities to develop and practice using these very different kinds of social-emotional communication skills in order to enact the three types of self-advocacy successfully.

Supporting Students' Listening Skills

The skill of listening is foundational for nearly every social interaction. Adept listeners follow a conversation receptively and absorb its ideas without interrupting in order to engage with that conversation more productively. Often, you can spot effective listeners by the facial expressions they use and the subvocal murmurs, nods, and body language that indicate they are paying attention and absorbing what's being said. Bailey (1993) identifies eight specific response types that listeners use.

1. *Addressing a personal reference to the speaker.* This entails using the speaker's name or the pronoun *you* in a response (e.g., "Great idea, Alex. You hit the nail on the head!").

2. *Referencing what a speaker has said.* For example, when Victor says, "I can't wait for lunch," it's clear Malia was listening when she responds, "I'm hungry, too."

3. *Making conversational references across all interactions.* It's powerful when someone we are talking with notices and affirms how we are feeling. For example, when Tatiana says, "I hear what you are saying. I felt bad too," Sophia responds, "Yes, I felt bad for him." Then Marcus adds, "He is so sad."

4. *Giving an evaluative response.* This type of response connects what's been said with a judgment—positive or negative (e.g., "I don't agree with you, because . . ." or "I agree with you, because . . .").

5. Not *responding.* One of the key components of any type of listening is showing that we have heard what a speaker says. But the truth is that in some situations, people will choose not to respond. For example, no one responded after Sophia said, "I have an idea. Let's skip doing a word problem and just add the stuff up." A nonresponse of any sort can mean many things, from disagreement and a lack of enthusiasm for an idea, to an indication that no one is really listening.

6. *Meaning negotiation.* Here, a listener asks for clarity or more information to develop a common understanding of something. For example, Pia asks Mrs. Nieves to explain the math homework and follows up with a lot of questions to help her understand what her teacher is saying.

7. *Collaborative completion of a sentence or phrase.* This occurs when a listener speaks up to complete or extend what one or more previous speakers have said. For example, when Mrs. Nieves provides her students with a sentence strip that says, "My favorite season is [blank] because . . . ," Kiarra responds with "My favorite season is winter because I like playing in the snow," and then Daniel adds, "Yes, I like it when it's cold."

8. *Back-channel responses.* In many conversations, listeners provide verbal signals that they are attending to what is being said with comments such as "Uh-huh" and "Yeah."

Each of these types of verbal exchanges requires students to be adept at using subtle yet critical self-expression skills when participating in a conversation. As these skills are being developed and strengthened, students must also work on expressing themselves clearly.

Supporting Students' Self-Expression Skills

Figure 7.6 lists some of the contexts in which self-advocacy skills are used to express an idea in a classroom setting. It also includes where and how particular skills can be supportively developed by teachers.

Some students may feel that school is not a welcome place to express their desires because they think of it as a place where rules must be followed and a place where students are subordinate to teacher authority. While it's likely that, in principle, all educators value students' self-advocacy and self-expression, especially when they do so in concert with explaining, extending, and strengthening concepts we are teaching, the reality of having a student express a need or desire, especially if it disrupts class or upsets the status quo, can be difficult for some of us to handle. Often the specifics of what one student needs for his/her process of understanding may not apply to the whole class. For example, a student who wants to interject a list of possible "what ifs" might easily slow down the process of giving directions so that everyone else can get to work. It's best to give such a student time to address their concerns one on one at another time. Similarly, students will vary in their willingness to contribute or advocate for their unique ideas if they're aware that their perspectives differ from their teacher's and if they've gotten pushback in the past. Some will jump at the chance to challenge the teacher's point of view; others shrink from the prospect.

Indeed, knowing how to effectively express one's ideas, needs, and desires is one of the greatest skills that a learner can have. What it offers is the freedom to express

FIGURE 7.6

Strategies to Build Self-Advocacy Skills: Expressing Ideas

Skill	Strategies
Express an idea about an area of study, such as a mathematical concept, to extend, clarify, or affirm an idea	Modeling, mini-lesson, in-the-moment interaction
Express an alternative or opposing idea in an area of study	Private advisory conference
Suggest an idea to resolve a dispute	Teaching and practicing conflict resolution protocols
Suggest an idea for self-empowerment, such as using one's voice to express a choice or preference for the way a concept is learned	Private advisory conference

oneself in ways that are meaningful and powerful. Lacking the ability to self-advocate puts a learner in the position of being a passive recipient of the ideas and attitudes of others instead of someone who is actively formulating and expressing ideas and attitudes of his or her own. In many cases (and certainly in the context of a democratic society), if students remain silent or passive about issues of importance that are failing to meet their needs, it can lead to negative feelings, ranging from being slightly upset to serious depression, and harmful outcomes, such as a student who does not ask for challenge remaining unchallenged, and a student who does not speak out about abuse continuing to be abused.

Figure 7.7 lists skills that students can apply to express needs. It also includes where and how teachers can supportively help them develop these skills.

Let's consider the example of Jaden, a 3rd grader who has become prone to frustrated outbursts that are becoming more severe and unpredictable and beginning to endanger his friendships. At recess, Jaden's teacher, Ms. Vasquez, observed him approaching a group of friends who were already involved in a game. "What are you doing!" he shouted. "No one is listening to me! Everyone in this school hates me!"

FIGURE 7.7

Strategies to Build Self-Advocacy Skills: Expressing Needs

Skills	Strategies
Ask for materials, help, or a turn to speak	Modeling, mini-lesson, in-the-moment interaction
Join a conversation, make or be a friend	Private advisory conference
Create boundaries for emotional safety	Teaching and practicing conflict resolution protocols, private advisory conference
Clarify a teacher's expectations or directions	Mini-lesson, one-on-one conversation
Speak up for a student's needs in partnerships	Modeling, mini-lesson, coaching
Speak up for a student's needs in a peer group, small group, or whole class	Modeling, mini-lesson, coaching
Speak up for another student's needs to school administration	Conversation with family and/or student (depending on student's age and the circumstances of the need)

Curious and concerned, Ms. Vasquez approached Jaden. "Looks like a tough recess, Jaden," she said. "May I walk with you a little?"

He shrugged, and she fell into step with him. They walked, briskly at first, but soon Jaden's pace slowed. Ms. Vasquez said, "Jaden, it looked to me like you wanted to play with them and they didn't see you at first. May I tell you a story?"

Jaden didn't say yes, but he appeared to be listening, so Ms. Vasquez continued. "I was new at a school once when I was in 3rd grade. I wanted to make friends, but it seemed like everyone already had friends. I was mad about that, and I didn't talk to anyone at first. They thought that because I looked mad, I didn't want to play. What I didn't realize was that if I knew how to ask to play with them in a calm way, they would have said yes. After I made my first friend, I told her how hard it was to get people to play. She said, 'We thought you didn't want to play because you were mad at us!' Isn't that weird? I would have never thought that."

"Really?" Jaden asked.

"Really. You want to try an experiment? See those boys over there playing ball? If you go over there, and, ask, with a calm voice, if it's OK if you join the game, I bet they'll let you play. But you can't have a frown. It has to be a smile or at least a regular face. Try it. I'll be right here."

Jaden carried out the experiment. As soon as he made his request, he was invited into the game. Later, in the classroom, Ms. Vasquez talked with him and reflected on the difference between Jaden's two attempts to join friends at recess, and what ideas he might take from this.

What this example illustrates is that mini-conferences don't have to be formal or classroom based. Still, they *are* lessons, and you can plan them as needed for a wide variety of skills that students might need, based on your observations. Think of the child who is nearsighted, cannot read the whiteboard, and doesn't know how to communicate that she is not benefiting from the support that her peers' and teacher's visual notations are offering. Think of the child who wants to move and run but stays seated because he doesn't want to "get in trouble." A pattern of silence or passivity can easily result in a lifetime of difficulty. Intervention from you, aimed at encouraging self-advocacy, can be tremendously powerful.

Unfortunately, self-advocacy is not something that can be mastered after a word or two of encouragement, a quick lesson, or even a series of lessons. What students need is the accumulation of myriad comprehensive learning experiences that help them develop a capstone of foundational skills over a sustained period of time.

Another set of self-advocacy skills every student needs are those that help express a desire for growth or responsibility. Sometimes students express such a desire directly, but in many cases, it might be a matter of recognizing and supporting a student's leadership potential with opportunities and then offering encouragement or a chance for reflection after he or she has exercised it on a more limited scale. Figure 7.8 shows the skills associated with expressing a desire as well as where and how we can support students' efforts to master them.

Students are constantly trying to find a balance between their own needs and the larger needs of the group. This search takes some students in the direction of assertiveness and others toward receptivity. (Of course, at different times, the emphasis may change.) Most adjust as they go, never reaching or achieving a permanent "just right" balance. The path to achieving an equitable balance begins with an honest inquiry into what they want and what motivates them. It also involves students being able to articulate desires and motivators and sharing this with others.

FIGURE 7.8

Strategies to Build Self-Advocacy Skills: Expressing a Desire

Skills	Strategies
Support an idea, a goal, or a practice	Modeling, mini-lesson, in-the-moment interaction
Take a leadership role	Modeling, mini-lesson, private advisory conference, in-the-moment interaction
Mediate a conflict or disagreement	Teaching and practicing mediation techniques
Facilitate a discussion	Teaching and practicing facilitation techniques, private advisory conference
Teach others	Teaching and practicing teaching techniques, private advisory conference
Coach or mentor someone	Teaching and practicing coaching/mentoring techniques, private advisory conference
Advocate for others	Teaching and practicing advocacy techniques, private advisory conference

Understanding what one needs and communicating honestly to others takes both self-awareness and courage. One way to support students' growth in this area is to begin by stressing that an effective self-advocate is one who is willing to continuously examine and assess the situations they find themselves in.

Teachers can build strategies for promoting self-advocacy by asking ourselves a series of *what, who, when, where,* and *how* questions about our students' needs. Figure 7.9 shows the types of questions we can ask to prepare ourselves for the work of building students' self-advocacy skills, as well as a few strategies to apply in the classroom.

Taking time to think through the steps we will take to plan a rich lesson or unit on student empowerment can help us create multiple opportunities for students to learn how to raise their own voices and advocate on behalf of themselves and others.

FIGURE 7.9

Planning Self-Advocacy Instruction: Questions and Strategies

Question Type	Planning Questions	Strategies
What	What does this student need to accomplish his or her goal? What supports does this student need to name and describe what he or she needs and desires?	Help students name what they need or desire—for example: −Information about class requirements −Assistance from a classroom aide −Support for a sensory need (e.g., "Can I sit away from the radiator?") −Clarification on a concept or skill
Who	Who is most likely to have what this student needs as well as the power, knowledge, or ability to provide it? Who is in charge or is most likely to be knowledgeable and helpful? Who is a trusted resource this student can go to for information, direction, and support? (Note: These resources might be yourself, another staff member, a peer partner, or a trained peer coach.)	Help students identify who they can go to for help—for example: −A peer who can demonstrate how to begin an assignment −A designated teacher who can demonstrate how to prepare a paper Stress that the simplest and most direct solution is usually the one to try first.

Question Type	Planning Questions	Strategies
When	When do I think it is appropriate for students to ask a question or express a need? —When is it OK and not OK to interrupt someone else? —When is it OK and not OK to correct someone else? —When is polite/impolite or constructive/disruptive to express feelings and opinions? —When is it OK and not OK to ask someone to give you their full attention? When will students be expected to practice self-advocacy?	Help students identify when is the right or wrong time to correct or interrupt someone. Help students know when it is acceptable to identify feelings and opinions and provide them with models of what this looks like (e.g., "May I sit with you at lunch?"). Help students understand when it is impolite or disruptive to express their feelings and opinions. Give students advance notice and reminders of circumstances when they are encouraged to speak up and express their ideas, needs, and desires.
Where	Where should students go to discuss various topics (e.g., the classroom, the counselor's office)?	Help students identify the right location to engage in self-advocacy for public and personal needs, desires, and ideas. Help students understand where it is acceptable to engage in a private conversation to self-advocate. Encourage the student to select a location that is comfortable for them too. Explain the reasons for choosing one location over another.
How	How can students best express themselves in various informal and formal situations? How much detail and background should students share when interacting with others?	Help students identify how to express themselves in formal and informal situations in school and elsewhere (e.g., in class, on the playground, in the cafeteria).
	How much should students say about their learning differences and exceptionality?	Help students know how and whether to share their differences with peers and others. Create scenarios of what this might look like in practice, including the risks and benefits. Support the student in developing their own informed choice of what to share and to whom, especially if the student has a learning disability, difference, or exceptionality

Larry Ferlazzo is a high school English and social studies teacher in Sacramento, California. He is also a contributor to *Education Week*. Larry provides us with an example of how he helped his students explore ways to advocate for change in their local community.

 Take a Closer Look: Preparing for Student Empowerment

The assignment for each student in two of my high school English classes was to have conversations with 10 other people—a mix of family members, students in our class, students in other classes, and at least one adult who was not part of their family. Their goal was to learn about the hopes and dreams that each had for their lives (both short and long term) and about their community concerns.

After completing 500 of these individual meetings, students had identified five primary community concerns: getting a good job, needing affordable housing, passing the U.S. citizenship test, fearing crime in their neighborhood, and obtaining a driver's license—with jobs being the biggest one.

As a next step, students learned about how community organizers distinguished between a problem and an issue. A problem was big and difficult to resolve. An issue was specific and achievable in a short period of time. Students formed small groups and worked together to develop ways to frame issues out of the problems they had identified.

The classes concluded they wanted to take some kind of action, so they focused on job training issues. They researched the different job training agencies and opportunities in the community, including meeting with a staff person at an agency located two blocks away. They learned that his organization was part of a consortium of similar agencies, and he agreed to bring representatives from all of them to a meeting at the school that the students would organize.

Students role-played all the different needed leadership roles and contacted all the people they had spoken with. More than 150 people attended this student-led meeting, and many followed up with job opportunities.

That same semester, we spent several class periods preparing for the U.S. citizenship test. Afterward, we discussed the attributes of a good citizen. This paragraph from Pao was typical of what students wrote:

A good citizen is someone who helps the community and makes the community better....I think organizing the meeting helped me prepare to be a good citizen more than studying for the citizenship test because I learned how to solve the community's problems and I know how to help the community.

—Larry Ferlazzo, English and social studies teacher, Luther Bank High School, Sacramento, California

 Time for Reflection

Describe two or three steps Larry's students took to identify the hopes, dreams, and concerns of their community. How did they use this information to develop an action plan for addressing these?

* * * * *

In the next chapter, we discuss expanding our involvement with family and community partners to explore how we can help students use their voice in real-world contexts, giving them an active and central role as empowered learners.

Extending Voice to Families and Communities

Partnerships with families and the larger community—individuals, agencies, and institutions—are valuable and sometimes overlooked resources for fostering student empowerment. Not only do parents and family members enlarge the circle of meaningful interactions that students can engage in to benefit their social-emotional and academic development and well-being, but they also strengthen our collective efforts to support students as autonomous beings. It's helpful and influential for students to see models of empowerment in and out of school (e.g., at home and in their community) and for students' work to be validated by the involvement, attention, and care of others beyond the classroom.

Consider a 4th grade student whose parents send him to public school and involve him in a variety of after-school activities, such as dance, soccer, music and art classes, and scouts. On the weekend, this 4th grader visits relatives, attends church, goes out to movies, and occasionally goes skiing. During the summer, his parents sign him up for various town-sponsored children's activities. All these interactions with the world make for a rich and busy life, and they encourage this little boy's social, cultural, intellectual, and communicative growth.

It's likely these activities are familiar to you, either because you engaged in them when you were a child, or you engage your own children in similar activities now. At work, maybe you have referred to these experiences to help your students connect to the curriculum, taking for granted that these activities will be as familiar to them as they are to you. However, as the demographic characteristics and cultural experiences of student and family populations become more diverse, these are assumptions educators would be wise to check. An example is a child who lives with his grandmother in an urban area beset with gang violence. The child's grandmother prefers to keep her grandson at home to allay her and his ongoing fear that he could be harmed.

U.S. Department of Education officials Bega, Johnson, and Jasper (2012) emphasize the need for schools to re-envision the ways in which they engage families and community members for the purpose of creating meaningful and sustained partnerships. It's a challenge that presents educators with a valuable opportunity to enhance our understanding of our students and gain insight that will make our instruction more responsive and more relevant. For those of us who are committed to student empowerment, forging connections with families is also a way to enhance our students' understanding of themselves—what they value, what they want, what they have to contribute, and why that matters.

In this chapter, we will explore the following topics:

- **Forging family partnerships.** These connections allow us to enlist families in building inclusive solutions to common problems.
- **Empowering all families to better empower all students.** Parents are models of empowerment for their children.
- **Using family-inclusive events as a forum for student empowerment.** In addition to being a way to strengthen connections between home and school, this allows us to center and celebrate the knowledge, interests, and ideas of students and families.
- **Enhancing school–community partnerships.** Providing opportunities for students to use their voice in real-world contexts gives them central role as empowered learners with responsibility, autonomy, and agency.

Forging Family Partnerships

Over the past few decades, the number of U.S. students below the poverty line has grown, ethnic diversity of the population has increased markedly, single-parent and blended families have become more common, and advances in technology have changed communications. Yet many educators' methods of engaging with parents have largely remained the same (Cohn & Caumont, 2016). We carry on with the traditional rituals and routines established years ago, in times of greater homogeneity.

Parent–teacher conferences, for example, have a particular rhythm, language of discourse, and routine that privilege those who are familiar with them. Parents are expected to show up at their child's school at an appointed time to listen to the teacher report their child's progress, often couched in a professional language of assessment scores, executive function, and social-emotional learning. Undoubtedly, the common forms and rituals for teacher–parent/guardian engagement, such as parent–teacher conferences and back-to-school or curriculum nights, are influenced by the reality that the vast majority of educators are white and middle class (Hollins & Guzman, 2005; U.S. Department of Education, 2016). The language and routines used at these events, part of a self-affirming professional culture, are doubly familiar to the white educators who grew up surrounded by them. White educators with limited firsthand experience with families who are culturally different from themselves may be insensitive to how intimidating or unfamiliar the routines and rituals of parent–teacher conferences and back-to-school nights may be to outsiders (Zacarian & Silverstone, 2015). Exacerbating this experience gap even further is the reality that most educators are trained at institutions of higher education by full-time faculty who also are mostly white (National Center for Education Statistics, 2019b). In addition, "Few teacher education institutions help candidates develop their knowledge, skills, and dispositions for family–school partnerships" (Walker & Dotger, 2012, p. 71). Indeed, many teachers share that they have had little training in working with families and are not quite sure how to engage parents, especially those who are different from themselves (Ferrara & Ferrara, 2005). When placed in the field for the first time, few preservice educators have contact with families, and many have a negative perception that parents don't care about their child's education (Moon & Neville, 2017). All of these limits and restrictions can reinforce practices that are ineffective at securing parent involvement despite educators knowing how valuable that involvement is.

What we must never forget is that parents are typically their child's greatest advocates, and the historical record shows myriad examples of what can result from ensuring they are empowered participants in school matters. Public education in the United States has been shaped by a variety of civil rights court cases characterized by parents fighting to secure their children's rights to an equal education—among them *Brown v. Board of Education of Topeka, Lau v. Nichols,* and *Pennsylvania Association for Retarded Children v. Commonwealth of Pennsylvania* (Hiatt, 1994). Many of these court cases have led to rulings that require schools to provide families with formal steering roles. For example,

> Project Head Start in 1964 for disadvantaged children in the inner cities and the Elementary and Secondary Education Act of 1965 required that parents serve on school advisory boards and participate in classroom activities and the Education for All Handicapped Act in 1974 required parents be an active partner in determining their child's educational program . . . [and] was to be developed by teacher, parent, child and specialists. (Hiatt, 1994, p. 255)

As we tap into the potential of parent/family partnerships, we understand that we must do so with curiosity, interest in each student's world, humility (in the face of the parents' challenges and their love for their children), and a commitment to work empathetically with families who are different from ourselves. These efforts are prerequisites to embracing diverse voices and, more important, to communicating to all students that their voices are valuable and powerful. Addressing the historic lack of diversity in the teaching ranks with active recruitment of teachers of diverse backgrounds and increased multicultural awareness on the part of all educators is an essential first step. But a valuable second one is to empower all families to have a voice by enlisting them as our partners in their child's education.

Consider the example of a high school teacher who knows that some of her students' families fled their homes in Puerto Rico and moved to her community in Florida as a result of Hurricane Maria. Overwhelmed with sympathy for her students, she can only see their experience through what they lost. She observes the group sitting alone in the cafeteria and tells them that they can come to her class-room to eat with her during lunch. They join her for the next two weeks. She feels she is providing them with a safe haven. She then gets a call from one of their parents. Through a translator, the parent tells the teacher that her child should not be eating in her classroom and should return to the cafeteria "like everyone else" and that "her daughter has much to contribute to her peers if she is given the chance." Rather than feel threatened and perceive this call as hostile, the teacher knows she has to be open and willing to listen carefully and with curiosity to identify the beliefs that shaped the parent's admonition, including that the teacher was not supporting or enabling the student to be empowered to take control over her life. It is important (though challenging) to remain open and curious to this type of call even though it might initially feel hurtful.

Broadening our vision of student empowerment and school–family partner-ships is an important goal. Just as we need to develop a more nuanced and informed understanding of our student populations, we must do the same with families. In Chapter 1, we looked at how being attuned to diversity involves taking steps to get to know students personally, socially, and culturally so that we may build relationships and instructional programs based on these understandings. The same holds true with building relationships with students' families. School–family relationship expert Joyce Epstein (2011) says we must care for families in the same way we care for their children. This can be done by conveying the following messages to families:

- We believe it's important to get to know one another.
- We value your participation.
- We want to work together.
- We are comfortable and embrace your involvement (Zacarian & Silverstone, 2015).

Further, building home–school relationships calls for educators to move away from a deficit-based way of thinking that assumes, for example, that poor families cannot care for their children appropriately; that poor families do not value educa-tion; or that families who do not speak English at home cannot support their child's English acquisition. Doing so means consciously accepting that (1) we don't know the assets and strengths of all families; (2) we must take steps to acquire the knowledge we know we don't yet have; and (3) we must engage in professional practices informed by our new understandings to such a degree that enacting them becomes second nature.

The same teacher from the previous example recently began working with a student from Guatemala who had once been detained at the U.S. border with his family. The family was struggling financially due to a layoff and coping with the stress of a grandfather's terminal illness. Having internalized the belief that all her students' families have strengths and assets that she's unaware of, the teacher now asks questions to solicit information about what her students may be experiencing at home, and she is open to learning more when she sees a student facing a challenge. She uses the asset-based questions in Figure 8.1 to guide her inquiry.

FIGURE 8.1

Suggested Meeting Topics to Build Family Partnerships

Topics	Questions
Qualities and values that make the student unique to their family	What makes [name of child] special (things that set them apart from others, qualities they have, things they value)?
What makes the relationship special between the parent and the student	What are some things you enjoy about [name of child]?
Qualities and values the parent appreciates from the student	What particular talents and skills would you like me to know about [name of child]?
Subjects that the student particularly likes and why they like these	What subjects does [name of child] like studying at home and in school, and what does she/he like about them?
The family's values and how they share their life together	What are things you enjoy doing as a family?
The family's likes and strengths	We want to be a welcoming place for you and your children. What would make the experience of coming to our school more enjoyable?
Partnership and collaboration that value the family's input	We see parents as our partners. Is there any particular way you would like to help me make [name of child's] school experience a great one?

(continued)

FIGURE 8.1 (cont.)

Suggested Meeting Topics to Build Family Partnerships

Topics	Questions
Ways the family was involved in their child's prior schooling	In what ways were parents encouraged to be involved at [name of child's] prior school?
Partnership and collaboration that leverages the family's assets	What special talents or interests would you consider sharing with the students in [name of child's] class or with students' families (e.g., work, interests, hobbies)?
The family's values and dreams for the student	What are your hopes and dreams for [name of child's] education?
Honesty, trust, partnership, and collaboration, along with a clear message of inclusiveness and belonging	What questions do you wish I had asked and would you like to be sure are included?

Source: Adapted from *Teaching to Strengths: Supporting Students Living with Trauma, Violence, and Chronic Stress* (p. 118) by D. Zacarian, L. Alvarez-Ortiz, & J. Haynes, 2017, Alexandria, VA: ASCD. Copyright 2017 by ASCD.

As we discussed in earlier chapters, we must foster conditions in which every encounter with families is unconditionally accepting, aimed at building a trust-based relationship, and expected to have a positive outcome for our goal of empowering students.

Empowering All Families to Better Empower All Students

Given the demands placed on educators, it's understandable that we would turn to a familiar core group of school-involved families when we need support for classroom, school, and district initiatives and activities. These parents are the natural go-tos, for example, when a school district representative is looking to add a parent member to a committee. The parents we already know and who are used to being called upon are very often the parents we empower further—and it's their children who experience their parents as models of empowerment. What we need to do is to find ways to involve the parents we don't yet know, those whose perspectives have not yet been considered, so that they too can become models of empowerment for their children. Here is an example that shows how challenging this work can be.

Take a Closer Look: Reflection of a Bilingual Bicultural School–Family Liaison

At a school staff meeting about engaging more families in events, a bilingual, bicultural school–family liaison (we'll call him Steve) shared a personal example. He and members of his family came to the United States in the late 1970s shortly after they had directly experienced the brutal tragedy of the Cambodian genocide. He told us that while his parents were satisfied that he was happy attending school, they never visited his school, even for his high school graduation. They told him that they felt school was not a place for them. He added that he became a school–family liaison to find ways to build close partnerships between schools and students' families. His experience sensitized him to the importance of family involvement and families having a voice in their child's education.

Time for Reflection

Imagine the school that Steve attended when he was a child.

1. What steps should have been taken to enlist his parents' participation in school events?
2. How might these events have been targeted to Steve's parents in order to help them partner with the teacher to promote his success in school?

Educational scholars and researchers Kim and Bryan (2017) found that while "parent empowerment may operate differentially for parents of various backgrounds," it has a significant impact on students' social-emotional health and academic success (p. 168). Their findings underscore the importance of fostering parent engagement in their child's education as a means of supporting student empowerment. In the work of Henderson, Jacob, Kernan-Schloss, and Raimondo (2004); Henderson, Mapp, Johnson, and Davies (2007); Epstein (2011); and Ferrara and Ferrara (2005), we find additional support for the criticality of finding ways to work with all of a school's families in order to support empowerment efforts. Henderson and colleagues (2007) use the term *partnerships* to describe what can occur when we work collaboratively with families, when we move from being "all-knowing" issuers of information, observations, conclusions, data, and assessment results to more of a partnership with families dedicated to the growth and well-being of students. As we have underscored throughout this book, promoting such partnerships requires continuous effort to build and sustain a strong sense of mutual trust, value, confidence, and competence in each other. An important first step is using a strengths-based approach in which we ensure that parents/guardians feel the same four essentials that we want students to experience: that they feel safe, a sense of belonging, acknowledged, and competent. To develop and sustain lasting and mutually fulfilling partnerships, we must take a strengths-based approach, valuing the resources and assets that all families possess, and work relentlessly to support family involvement with schools (Saint-Jacques, Turcotte, & Pouliot, 2009).

Within this paradigm, there are overarching questions that should guide educators' efforts to work with families:

1. How can I keep parents/guardians continuously informed of what their child is doing well?
2. How can I express this even in the smallest ways to celebrate the successes of their child?
3. How can I support families to celebrate the assets, strengths, and resources they bring to their child's learning (Zacarian et al., 2017)?

As an example of how a teacher can start using a strengths-based approach to empower families and, by extension, students, consider Mrs. Banks, whose class is preparing student-led conferences for their families. She begins by asking them to think about which of their projects or assignments represents their best work—successes they can highlight. When she notices a student named William sitting still with his pencil in the air, she pulls him aside for a quick conversation. William states matter-of-factly that compared to his classmates, he's not very successful; he doesn't have any impressive work to show—no A-graded projects or 100-percent test scores. Mrs. Banks sits with William for a few minutes going through his portfolio. She prompts him to find examples of his progress and growth, and she affirms these as accomplishments worth sharing with his parents.

Time for Reflection

1. If you were Mrs. Banks, what are some ways that you might invite students to notice ways that their work shows their personal growth?
2. How might you create opportunities to make this reflective self-assessment more empowering for your students?

Holding Student-Led Conferences

We first mentioned student-led conferences in Chapter 5, suggesting them as opportunities for students to share their learning with their teacher and families and, more important, be empowered to lead an event and take an authoritative role. We provided eight considerations for planning, engaging in, and reflecting on the success of these events (see pp. 99–100). One involves inviting families. The goal is to provide a welcoming invitation that sparks family interest in attending the event and affirming a date, time, and place that works for them. In Figure 8.2, you'll find a sample invitation adapted from Berger and colleagues (2014).

 Time for Reflection

1. Review Figure 8.2. Create your own invitation for a student-led conference, making it as welcoming as possible.
2. Discuss two to three activities you could create to ensure that you increase your response rate as much as possible. To get you started, one idea is to use the letter as a script to reach out to former families to ask that they help you in getting the word out about the positive experiences they had attending their child's student-led conference.

Using Family Dialogue Journals and Interviews

Student, family, and teacher interactions can also be promoted through family dialogue journals (FDJs) and interviews. There are three core aspects of FDJs: they must be "linked to student learning, . . . support student learning at home, and . . . build respectful relationships with all families" (Allen et al., 2015, p. 4). Along with extending students' interactions on topics related to what they are learning, there are

FIGURE 8.2

Sample Invitation for Student-Led Conference

Dear Families,

I am looking forward to working with you, your child, and our class community! I am writing to share an exciting activity that we will be doing this year: student-led conferences. Our goal is to provide students with an opportunity to share their learning and progress, show the projects that they have been working on, and receive positive feedback for their efforts.

Your child, his/her peers, and I are planning the event. We suggest the following date, time, and place for the conference.

Date: Time: Place:

Please let me know if the date, time, and place work for you. If not, please provide some alternative dates and times that do. You can email me at [e-mail address] or leave me a voicemail message at [phone number].

Thank you, and I am looking forward to working in partnership with you and your child!

Sincerely,

[Teacher's Name]

many additional benefits of FDJs. They help build a home–school connection so that families better understand what their child is learning in school and can contribute to the child's learning.

The intent of FDJs, according to Moll (2015), is for students, teachers, and families to "share personal details about their lives, experiences, and opinions" based on sentence prompts that relate to what students are studying (p. vii). Figure 8.3 provides some examples. Allen and colleagues (2015) share this view of family dialogue journals, cautioning that such written exchanges must be based on mutual and reciprocal trust. It is also important that they be written in a family's home language, when necessary, to encourage interaction. This means making a plan to arrange for translation.

FDJs can also be an excellent medium for families to share their thoughts with their children. According to Allen and colleagues (2015), these types of

FIGURE 8.3

Examples of Class-Created Prompts That Connect to the Curriculum

Topic	Family Dialogue Journal Prompt
In U.S. history class, high school students are analyzing the causes of the Revolutionary War.	This week, we learned about the causes of the Revolutionary War in the United States. Why do you think some countries go to war with others?
In science class, 4th grade students are learning how to find facts that are "proven" and not opinions.	This week, we have been learning about how to do an internet search to find proven facts instead of opinions. How have you learned to do that?
In English language arts class, middle school students are studying the concept of author's intent in order to understand the author's meaning and interpretation. They are currently reading *Rifles for Watie*, a fiction book that takes place during the U.S. Civil War.	Last week, we began reading about an ordinary soldier who fought in the Civil War. At one point in the story, he loses hope. Have you ever lost hope? If so, why?

conversations can really help students build "academic connections" and gain a deeper understanding of such critical concepts as cultural identity through exploring "family values, culture, opinions, and memories" (p. 18). They also put students in an expert position by offering explanation and understanding to their families and teachers. Figure 8.4 shows a sample letter inviting parents and guardians to participate in an FDJ.

We recommend that FDJ entries be written by hand in a single notebook, which allows all participants (the student, the family, you) to see all responses. It can also be helpful to provide models of FDJ responses, which can guide families to contribute in ways that are positive, supportive, and engaging. The FDJ that follows was written by a student and his grandmother.

> Dear Grandma,
>
> This week, we learned about the causes of the Revolutionary War in the United States. Why do you think some countries go to war with others? I think some countries go to war when they believe that their freedoms are being overtaken by an unreasonable ruler.
>
> Love,
>
> Bella

FIGURE 8.4

Sample Invitation for a Family Dialogue Journal

Dear Families,

I am writing to share an exciting activity that we will be doing this year. It is called a family dialogue journal. Our goal is to provide students, families, and me with an opportunity to share and contribute to what students are learning. Each month, our class will create a question about what they are learning, respond to that question, and then ask you and then me to also write a response. Our plan is to follow the sequence below using the same notebook throughout the semester so that we can read what each other writes:

Week 1: Students co-create a question with me.

Week 2: Students write a response and bring it home to you.

Week 3: You respond to the question and what they have written.

Week 4: I respond to the question and what students and you have written.

Here are the dates that the family dialogue journals will be sent home to you and then due to be returned:

Journal 1: [Date parents/guardians will receive it and date it is due]

Journal 2: [Date parents/guardians will receive it and date it is due]

Journal 3: [Date parents/guardians will receive it and date it is due]

Journal 4: [Date parents/guardians will receive it and date it is due]

Thank you, and I am looking forward to working in partnership with you and your child!

Sincerely,

[Teacher's Name]

Dear Bella,

When I was in high school in 1968, many of my friends fought in the war in Vietnam. Since so many died in that war, I often wonder why our country sent my friends and thousands of others there. At that time, we were told that we needed to go to war to protect the United States from becoming a communist country. I never understood that reason. I think it was just an excuse for us to fight a war that only the people in power in the government wanted. I think that most countries go to war for the same reasons as what we were told—when they fear that they will be taken over by another. Another cause is when a country is being governed by another and believes that they are being treated unfairly by that ruler.

Love,

Grandma

The general sequence of an FDJ targeted for student empowerment is to do it repeatedly throughout the school year at intervals that you, students, and parents/guardians as well as colleagues believe will work best (e.g., weekly, biweekly, monthly). Figure 8.5 depicts the sequence of events.

FIGURE 8.5

Sequence of Family Dialogue Journals

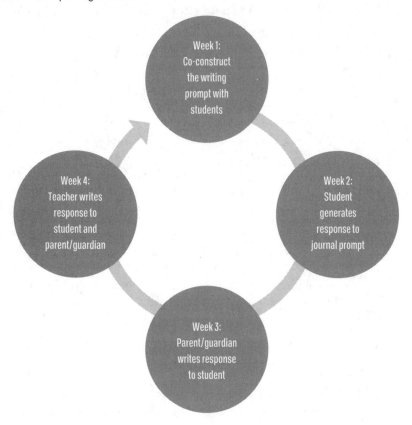

There may be parents/guardians who decline to participate for a variety of reasons. Rather than make them and their child feel excluded, try to secure alternate participants who can support the flow of interactions we want students to engage in. These might be a student's sibling or another relative or adult who provides the child with extrafamilial supports. It can also be a colleague in your school (e.g., specialist teacher, guidance counselor, teacher's aide) who is willing to be an adult respondent.

Similarly, there may be families who are interested but do not feel comfortable writing an FDJ response. The purpose of FDJs is to engage in conversation with a family to enhance the student's learning and the family's understanding of that learning. This can also be achieved through students interviewing a parent/guardian, family friend, or other caring adult. It is helpful for students to listen and then share what they have learned with their teacher. Young learners or pre-emergent writers can do this by drawing what they have learned. Students who possess early literacy skills can do this by writing a summary of what they have learned to share with their teacher, and then sharing with their families what their teacher has written.

Using Classroom-Based Family-Inclusive Events as a Forum for Student Empowerment

Classroom-based events can be ideal opportunities to amplify our goals to empower students. They put the spotlight on students and draw from the many resources and assets that they and their families can contribute. Based on our research and writing on this topic (Zacarian & Silverstone, 2015, 2017), we can classify these events into four broad categories:

1. Community-building events for social purposes
2. Showcasing the curriculum to make learning transparent
3. Drawing on the rich resources of families
4. Building a home–school culture of learning

While each has a different purpose, the overarching objective is to put the knowledge, interests, and ideas of students and families at the center of what is being recognized and celebrated.

Community-Building Events for Social Purposes

We believe in the importance of building partnerships early in the school year; this is especially important for families who may perceive schools to be unwelcoming or unfamiliar places. Similarly, relationship building is useful to those of us who might find the prospect of working with, let alone partnering with, families to be a stressful proposition. Inviting families to join us at social events can do two important things: (1) affirm the personal, social, and cultural collectivist ideologies that many families represent and (2) build positive momentum for the school year. Because they are created with students' collaborative input and creativity, both of these things are invaluable to our empowerment efforts. Examples include a family picnic, breakfast, or tea where families bring or share their own food; a dance that celebrates the cultural dances of the community; a game or art night; a welcome breakfast; or any other creative idea that ensures the full participation of families. Here are suggested preparatory steps for creating social events intended to build relationships with families.

1. *Plan collaboratively.* Plan events with students as well as colleagues (e.g., special education, ESL, bilingual, art, music, and subject matter teachers; other teachers and specialists), alumni families, members from the families' communities, and, of course, students. The goal of planning a social event with students at the center should be to best ensure the inclusive participation of every family.

2. *Schedule to maximize participation.* With students' input, select a start and end time and date to ensure the most participation. For example, some families may work evenings, making an event held before school begins more accessible to all. Hold at least one other event during the year before school, during the school day, immediately after school, or in the early evening for families who are not able to attend the time that is convenient to the majority.

3. *Get the administration involved.* Discuss in advance with school administration any prospective plans for social events that involve bringing families to a classroom or school. Always secure the administration's full, informed support before issuing any invitations.

4. *Make the invitations personal.* Have students create personal invitations for the event during the school day, in writing, online, or in artful signage so they can

develop their communications skills and be direct ambassadors to their families. With students, find families (e.g., alumni, volunteers) who will reach out to personally to invite others.

5. *Make sure event announcements reach intended recipients and can be understood.* Enlist students' support to translate and disseminate written notices about the event into the languages spoken by students' families, taking steps to make sure these notices reach families who might not have e-mail or phone service.

6. *Don't rely on a single mode of communication.* Try to reach families multiple ways with the announcement of any event. Don't assume that one mention in a newsletter will be enough to cut through the clutter of busy lives. Student involvement in getting the word out is key.

7. *Take steps to help all attendees feel welcome.* Position student greeters at the door to engage families in social conversations, bring them personally to the event, and ensure that they feel at home throughout.

Showcasing the Curriculum to Make Learning Transparent

Curriculum events are great opportunities for children to be empowered to share with their families and others what they have learned or are learning. Students should have a decision-making role in the event, which can take a variety of forms, from a debate, a poetry slam, or a poster presentation to plays and other creative performance ideas. The aim is to encourage and support the highest level of student engagement and family participation. Curriculum showcase events involve the same seven preparatory steps as planning community-building events for social purposes, but there are few additional considerations to keep in mind.

1. *Remember the event's purpose.* Curriculum showcase events are opportunities for students to demonstrate their learning and receive public acknowledgment and validation.

2. *Let students decide how to show themselves in their best light.* Provide multiple opportunities for students to be involved in choosing the type of presentation event they believe will work best for them.

3. *Provide practice time and feedback on performance in progress.* Give students ample opportunities to practice their presentations or performance with peers

and others so that they will be better prepared for the actual event. If possible, use video as a way to rehearse and identify areas that may need improvement. The more students are able to reflect on and become self-aware of what they are doing, the easier it will be for them to take responsibility for the excellence of their presentation and feel a sense of pride in its completion.

4. *Build time for feedback and recognition into the event itself.* Make sure the actual event includes time for families to acknowledge and recognize what students have accomplished and showcased.

Drawing on the Rich Resources of Families

All families have a wide array of resources, talents, and assets to share with classroom and school communities. They can bring connections to or perspectives on content that are personal or professional, cultural/linguistic, and social.

Each time an adult from beyond the classroom offers a presentation to students, it is a powerful statement of caring. It says, "The work you do in school is important enough for me to give of my time as an adult. What you see me doing in my life and career is also possible for you to do since I am from your community." This is an invaluable and empowering seed of future possibility. Adult presenters are role models who potentially raise the ceiling for what students imagine they might be empowered to become. They allow young people to rehearse possibilities and normalize achievement.

These presenters also offer acknowledgment and recognition of the cultures and families that students come from. When adults who look like them or look like their culturally different peers are given a place of respect and authority to share something of value to all, the status of all families is transformed into an asset and a source of strength. This is particularly true among students who would otherwise feel their home cultures exist outside, unseen by the school community.

When families come to our classrooms, we should prepare them in whatever ways they believe will help and share with them information about our classroom population (e.g., total number of students and adults in the class, start and end times of the activity). Here are some suggested steps to take.

1. *Explain the purpose or goal of having a family member visit and present.* For example, a parent who is a plumber might be invited to a high school chemistry

class to demonstrate how pipes are welded together—an authentic application of thermal reaction.

2. *Provide guidelines for the presenter.* It's important to share the start and end times, the total number of students and adults in the class, and any other pertinent information that will help a family member prepare for the visit.

3. *Offer to be a sounding board as family members plan presentations.* Your feedback at the planning stage can help the presenter fine-tune ideas and highlight content connections.

4. *Prepare students for family member visits.* As with any activity, it's helpful to build student interest and excitement. Review the purpose of each planned presentation and prompt students to brainstorm questions they would like to ask. Send a list of questions home with the student whose family member will be presenting so that he or she can might prepare responses.

5. *Co-create thank-you notes.* Always have students collaborate on and send a formal thank-you to every visiting presenter.

Building a Home–School Culture of Learning

We want to enable all families to be empowered as partners in their child's learning and to support their children to be empowered learners and citizens. Family curriculum events are a wonderful means to make what we are doing in school transparent. Again, these events involve the same seven steps listed earlier for community-based events for social purposes.

An example is a high school chemistry teacher who is helping students learn the principles behind chemical reactions. During a curriculum event, the teacher invites families and students to learn some of the key principles by exploring and observing firsthand the properties of thermal reaction in tying railroad rails together to form miles and miles of tracks (Zacarian et al., 2017).

Another example is an elementary school teacher who invites families in for a math game night where students can teach their families to play the learning games and activities that they practice in math workshop, thereby giving families insight into the methods and ideas that their children are learning. Such experiences help adults be insiders, making it possible to have and extend conversations about learning with their children at home (Zacarian & Silverstone, 2015).

Enhancing School–Community Partnerships

In addition to strengthening family involvement and partnerships, it is critical to create, strengthen, and sustain community partnerships to model ways students might be empowered to work with others to support a collective goal. Often, we find ourselves partnering with others outside the school to address the need for dental care or health care, the problem of food insecurity, and so forth. Reenvisioning these partnerships should take into account how individuals, agencies, and institutions can work reciprocally with students and educators to address a school or district need in a way that benefits all. These partnerships must be grounded in

- Students having a role in creation, implementation, and evaluation.
- Addressing a need.
- Developing a mutually sustainable and beneficial idea.
- Community partners having a voice and a choice in all that occurs.

Here are three examples of this type of re-envisioning:

1. A middle school wants to provide students with supported experiences using media-driven technology. A local public radio station wants to expand its audience to a younger population. The two engage in a partnership to support and air student podcasts.
2. A high school wants to support student entrepreneurship. A weekly local street fair wants to support its local community's business enterprises. The two engage in a partnership to provide students with exhibitor space to share projects.
3. An elementary school wants to create a community garden. A new local garden shop wants exposure as a positive contributor to the community. The two collaborate to build a community vegetable and fruit garden that is wholly based on students' ideas and explorations.

Such partnerships can be powerful when community partners have depth of understanding about the diversity among local student and family populations. They can also help our efforts to empower students to be more engaged in school and in their lives and for them to contribute to the service of others. To achieve this, we must tap into the tremendous possibilities that exist in our local communities.

Take a Closer Look: The Partnership Between Wolfe Street School and the University of Maryland School of Dentistry

An example of the type of school–community partnerships that we are referring to is the one that Wolfe Street School in Baltimore, Maryland, has with the University of Maryland's School of Dentistry (WETA Public Broadcasting, 2019b). Many Wolfe Street students had significant dental challenges that were impacting their health and well-being. The community school liaison identified a partner in the University of Maryland's School of Dentistry and worked closely with its director to expand the dental school's internship opportunities and care for the students (WETA Public Broadcasting, 2019a). And what started with providing dental interns with these opportunities and students with much-needed care has expanded: with help from the dental school, Wolfe Street's students provide peers with nutrition and dental hygiene support. Mutually beneficial partnership efforts such as this have been shown to address students' needs, support their desires and hopes, and, as essentially, put them in leadership positions.

Take a Closer Look: The Partnership Between the Escuela Ponce de León and Its Students' Families

The late 1980s were a harrowing time in Juan Domingo, a barrio in the town of Guaynabo, near San Juan, Puerto Rico. Explosive growth in the drug trade had led to social problems including widespread drug use, a spike in incarceration rates, and gang activity involving young people. After Hurricane Hugo in 1989, the government had slated the local schools for elimination (Ayer, 2018). According to Ana María García Blanco, the principal of Escuela Ponce de León since 1993, "The parents said, 'You can't close down our school, because that would be the end of our community.'" With volunteer effort, their children witnessed the restoration of the building, its reopening, and the creation of a publicly funded Montessori school. Ana María reflected on the significance of this:

> Shortly afterward there was an election. The next governor used the example of this school to help create a school reform law in 1993 that encouraged community decision making regarding schools, giving parents and families a central role. We developed a methodology in Juan Domingo and have improved it over time. It's a roundtable, a collective of people that

work together for the common good, and there is a code of honor that we all abide by for the good of the community.

So the action of the parents at our school not only had a powerful effect on the quality of life in their community but became an example to students, their families, and the general community that helped influence education policies throughout Puerto Rico.

In the time since the Escuela Ponce de León's reopening as a public Montessori school, more than 50 other public Montessori schools have opened in Puerto Rico. American Montessori Society 2017 Living Legacy honorees Michael Duffy and Rebecca D'Neil Duffy, who are cofounders of a Montessori Training Institute in Massachusetts, have worked with Ana María and others to help establish the Instituto Nueva Escuela to provide certification and training directly to Montessori teachers in Puerto Rico. They note:

> Each of the public Montessori schools in Puerto Rico has impacted the surrounding, mostly poor communities in which they are located. They have engaged parents in volunteering at the schools and even hired parents as classroom assistants, cooks, and janitors. For their part, students have become heavily involved in service projects in the communities. They have provided an oasis of peace for children growing up in violent neighborhoods and promoted a more peaceful community around them. After Hurricane Maria, the Montessori public school communities were among the first to organize themselves—students and parents—to repair the damage and reopen for classes, well before most of the other public schools. Whenever the Montessori programs in their schools are threatened by governmental actions, students and parents mobilize in support of the schools, staging protests, collecting petitions, and creating successful pressure campaigns to preserve their programs.

  Time for Reflection

1. Describe a partnership in which students would (a) address a need and (b) have a voice in creating, implementing, and evaluating a partnership.

2. Describe how you would ensure that the community partner would (a) value empowering students by giving them a voice and (b) see the mutual benefits in collaborating together.
3. What are some examples of community partnership that might extend benefits beyond the students into the community at large?

* * * * *

We began this book by discussing the need for students to have multiple opportunities to gain a sense of control and have a real voice in the decisions that affect their learning, their lives, and the lives of others. We described what educators can do to help students develop a personal understanding of the influence they can have in their classrooms, schools, communities, and beyond, and how we can enhance school–community partnerships. It takes time, energy, and commitment to build meaningful partnerships for our ever-changing student populations, but the rewards of creating these kinds of connections for student success can be energizing to our own practice, our profession, our society, and, of course, our students.

The world needs young people who are empowered to be self-directed and sensitively attuned to the needs of those around them so that they may contribute to the betterment of their communities and the world we share. For educators, there is no better time to renew our commitment to this work.

Acknowledgments

We want to express our gratitude to several people who contributed to this book.

ASCD acquisitions editor Susan Hills excitedly took the ideas that we had, suggested additional ones, and helped us craft them into this book.

Many educators from across the continental United States and Puerto Rico generously and graciously provided examples of their empowerment efforts. They include Ana María García Blanco, Robyn Breiman, Sandra Deacon, Marta Donohoe, Michael Duffy, Rebecca D'Neil Duffy, Larry Ferlazzo, Kevin Hodgson, Jennifer Hunter, Beth Jewell, William Maier, Sheila Reid, Christine Sand, and Nancy Turner.

Throughout the publication process, editor Katie Martin provided the meta and micro input that was needed, copyeditor Sarah Duffy made many corrections to polish our effort, and designer Donald Ely hand-created the beautiful cover.

A very special thanks goes to our spouses, children, and friends for their support throughout the writing project. Michael also wishes to thank his colleagues at Wellan Montessori School and at the Montessori Elementary Education Teacher Training Collaborative.

Finally, we dedicate this book to students and teachers. They show us how we can work and learn together to create a caring community in which everyone's potential is discovered and valued.

References

Alexander, K., & Alexander, M. D. (2011). *American public school law* (9th ed.). Belmont, CA: Wadsworth.

Allen, J., Beaty, J., Dean, A., Jones, J., Smith Mathew, S., McCreight, J., . . . Simmons, A. M. (2015). *Family dialogue journals: School–home partnerships that support student learning.* New York: Teachers College Press.

Anderson, M. D. (2016, April 26). How internet filtering hurts kids. *The Atlantic.* Retrieved from https://www.theatlantic.com/education/archive/2016/04/internet-filtering-hurts-kids/479907/

Ayer, D. (2018, February 8). Public Montessori in Puerto Rico. Retrieved from http://www.montessoripublic.org/2018/02/public-montessori-puerto-rico/

Bailey, F. M. (1993). *Voice in collaborative learning: An ethnographic study of a second language methods course* (Doctoral dissertation). Retrieved from https://scholarworks.umass.edu/dissertations/AAI9408253/

Baker, C., Wright, W. E., & Cook, B. J. (2017). *Foundations of bilingual education and bilingualism* (6th ed.). Blue Ridge Summit, PA: Multilingual Matters.

Baker, L. (2012, January). *A history of school design and its indoor environmental standards, 1900 to today.* Washington, DC: National Clearinghouse for Educational Facilities. Retrieved from http://www.ncef.org/pubs/greenschoolshistory.pdf

Bega, D., Johnson, J., & Jasper, C. (2012, February). *Rethinking Title I parental involvement: Moving beyond a checklist of activities to a systemic plan for sustained family and community engagement.* Paper presented at Georgia's Statewide Family Engagement Conference, Athens, GA.

Berger, R., Rugen, L., & Woodfin, L. (2014). *Leaders of their own learning: Transforming schools through student-engaged assessment.* San Francisco: Jossey-Bass.

Bernard, M., & Newell, E. P. (2013). Students affected by neglect. In E. Rossen & R. Hull (Eds.), *Supporting and educating traumatized students: A guide for school-based professionals* (pp. 203–217). New York: Oxford University Press.

Biswas-Dienera, R., Kashdan, T. B., & Gurpal, M. (2011). A dynamic approach to psychological strength development and intervention. *Journal of Positive Psychology, 6*(2), 106–118.

Blankstein, A. M., & Noguera, P. (2015). *Excellence through equity: Five principles of courageous leadership to guide achievement for every student.* Alexandria, VA: ASCD.

Blaustein, M. E. (2013). Childhood trauma and a framework for intervention. In E. Rossen & R. Hull (Eds.), *Supporting and educating traumatized students: A guide for school-based professionals* (pp. 3–21). New York: Oxford University Press.

Budge, K. M., & Parrett, W. H. (2018). *Disrupting poverty: Five powerful classroom practices.* Alexandria, VA: ASCD.

Calkins, L., Kloss, D., & Vanderburg, T. (2018). *A quick guide to getting started with units of study, K–8.* Portsmouth, NH: Heinemann.

Center for Responsive Schools. (2001, April 1). Classroom spaces that work. Retrieved from https://www.responsiveclassroom.org/classroom-spaces-that-work/

Center for Responsive Schools. (2015, November 3). Our classroom walls. Retrieved from https://www.responsiveclassroom.org/our-classroom-walls/

Centers for Disease Control and Prevention. (2018, August 8). Sleep and sleep disorders. Retrieved from https://www.cdc.gov/sleep/about_sleep/chronic_disease.html

Charney, R. S. (2002). *Teaching children to care: Management in the responsive classroom.* Greenfield, MA: Northeast Foundation for Children.

Cohen, D. K. (1988). *Teaching practice: Plus ça change.* East Lansing, MI: National Center for Research on Teacher Education.

Cohen, E. G., & Lotan, R. (2014). *Designing groupwork: Strategies for the heterogeneous classroom* (10th ed.). New York: Teachers College Press.

Cohn, D., & Caumont, A. (2016, March 31). 10 demographic trends that are shaping the U.S. and the world in 2016. Retrieved from http://www.pewresearch.org/fact-tank/2016/03/31/10-demographic-trends-that-are-shaping-the-u-s-and-the-world/

Costa, A. L. (2017). Foreword. In B. Kallick & A. Zmuda, *Students at the center: Personalized learning with Habits of Mind* (pp. ix–xi). Alexandria, VA: ASCD.

Court, A. (2010). The effects of exposure to natural light in the workplace on the health and productivity of office workers: A systematic review protocol. *JBI Library of Systematic Reviews, 8*(16), 1–19. doi: 10.11124/jbisrir-2010-574

Csikszentmihalyi, M. (1990). *Flow: The psychology of optimal experience.* New York: Harper & Row.

Curwin, R. (2010). *Meeting students where they live: Motivation in urban schools.* Alexandria, VA: ASCD.

DeBose, C. (1992). Codeswitching: Black English and standard English in the African-American linguistic repertoire. In C. M. Eastman (Ed.), *Codeswitching* (pp. 157–167). Bristol, UK: Multilingual Matters.

Delpit, L. (1995). *Other people's children: Cultural conflict in the classroom.* New York: New Press.

Denton, P. (2007). *The power of our words: Teacher language that helps children learn.* Greenfield, MA: Northeast Foundation for Children.

Dewey, J. (1938). *Experience and education.* New York: Collier Books.

Durlak, J. A., Weissberg, R. P., Dymnicki, A. B., Taylor, R. D., & Schellinger, K. B. (2011). The impact of enhancing students' social and emotional learning: A meta-analysis of school-based universal interventions. *Child Development, 82*(1), 405–432.

Dweck, C. (2006). *Mindset: The new psychology of success.* New York: Ballantine Books.

Dweck, C., Walton, G. M., & Cohen, G. L. (2014). *Academic tenacity: Mindsets and skills that promote long-term learning.* Retrieved from https://ed.stanford.edu/sites/default/files/manual/dweck-walton-cohen-2014.pdf

Edmondson, A. C. (2004, March). Learning from mistakes is easier said than done: Group and organizational influences on the detection and correction of human error. *Journal of Applied Behavioral Science, 40*(1), 66–90. doi: 10.1177/0021886304263849

Edwards, P. A., Domke. L., & White, K. (2017). Closing the parent gap in changing school districts. In S. B. Wepner & D. W. Gomez (Eds.), *Challenges facing suburban schools: Promising responses to changing student populations* (pp. 109–123). Lanham, MD: Rowman & Littlefield.

Epstein, J. (2011). *School, family, and community partnerships: Preparing educators and improving schools* (2nd ed.). Philadelphia: Westview Press.

Erikson, E. H., & Erikson, J. M. (1998). *The life cycle completed* (Extended version). New York: W. W. Norton.

Faison, C. L. (1996, September–October). Modeling instructional technology use in teacher preparation: Why we can't wait. *Educational Technology, 36*(5), 57–59.

Farmer, T., Chen, C., Hamm, J. V., Moates, M. M., Mehtaji, M., Lee, D., & Huenke, M. R. (2016, March). Supporting teachers' management of middle school social dynamics: The scouting report process. *Intervention in School and Clinic, 52*(2), 67–76.

Ferrara, M. M., & Ferrara, P. J. (2005, November/December). Parents as partners: Raising awareness as a teacher preparation program. *The Clearinghouse, 79*(2), 77–82.

Flores, R. L. (2017). The rising gap between rich and poor: A look at the persistence of educational disparities in the United States and why we should worry. *Cogent Social Sciences, 3.* doi: 10.1080/23311886.2017.1323698

Floyd, D. T., & McKenna, L. (2003). National youth organizations in the United States: Contributions to civil society. In D. Wertlieb, F. Jacobs, & R. M. Lerner (Eds.), *Handbook of applied developmental science: Promoting positive child, adolescent, and family development through research, policies, and programs* (pp. 11–26). Thousand Oaks, CA: Sage.

Fung, B. (2018, March 8). To get rural kids online, Microsoft wants to put internet access on school buses. Retrieved from https://www.washingtonpost.com/news/innovations/wp/2018/03/08/to-get-rural-kids-online-microsoft-wants-to-put-internet-access-on-school-buses/

Gabel, P. (2018). *The desire for mutual recognition: Social movements and the dissolution of the false self.* New York: Routledge.

Gauvain, M. (2001). *The social context of cognitive development.* New York: Guilford Press.

Gauvain, M. (2013). Sociocultural contexts of development. In P. D. Zelazo (Ed.), *Oxford handbook of developmental psychology: Vol. 2. Self and other* (pp. 425–451). New York: Oxford University Press.

Gonzalez, N., Moll, L. C., & Amanti, C. (Eds.). (2005). *Funds of knowledge: Theorizing practices in households, communities, and classrooms.* Mahwah, NJ: Lawrence Erlbaum.

Gordon, T. (2000). *Parent effectiveness training: The proven program for raising responsible children.* New York: Random House.

Gordon, T. (2016). Origins of the Gordon model. Retrieved from http://www.gordontraining.com/thomas-gordon/origins-of-the-gordon-model/

Gorski, P. C., & Pothini, S. G. (2018). *Case studies on diversity and social justice education* (2nd ed.). Boca Raton, FL: CRC Press.

Groskop, V. (2013, August 17). How to raise a creative child. *The Guardian.* Retrieved from https://www.theguardian.com/lifeandstyle/2013/aug/17/art-of-raising-creative-children

Henderson, A., Jacob, B., Kernan-Schloss, A., & Raimondo, B. (2004). *The case for parent leadership.* Lexington, KY: Primchard Committee for Academic Excellence.

Henderson, A. T., Mapp, K. L., Johnson, V. R., & Davies, D. (2007). *Beyond the bake sale: The essential guide to family partnerships.* New York: New Press.

Hertel, R., & Johnson, M. M. (2013). How the traumatic experiences of students manifest in school settings. In E. Rossen & R. Hull (Eds.), *Supporting and educating traumatized students: A guide for school-based professionals* (pp. 23–35). New York: Oxford University Press.

Hiatt, D. B. (1994). Parent involvement in American public schools: A historical perspective 1642–1994. *The School Community Journal, 4*(2), 27–38.

Hollins, E. R., & Guzman, M. T. (2005). Research on preparing teachers for diverse populations. In M. Cochran-Smith & K. M. Zeichner (Eds.), *Studying teacher education: The report of the AERA Panel on Research and Teacher Education* (pp. 477–548). Mahwah, NJ: Lawrence Erlbaum; and Washington, DC: American Educational Research Association.

Howard, J. (2016, July 29). Americans devote more than 10 hours a day to screen time, and growing. *CNN.* Retrieved from https://www.cnn.com/2016/06/30/health/americans-screen-time-nielsen/

Humes, K. R., Jones, N. A., & Ramirez, R. R. (2011, March). Overview of race and Hispanic origin: 2010. Retrieved from https://www.census.gov/prod/cen2010/briefs/c2010br-02.pdf

Jensen, E. (2009). *Teaching with poverty in mind: What being poor does to kids' brains and what schools can do about it.* Alexandria, VA: ASCD.

Johnson, D. W., & Johnson, F. (2009). *Joining together: Group theory and group skills* (10th ed.). Boston: Allyn and Bacon.

Johnson, D. W., Johnson, R., & Holubec, E. (2008). *Cooperation in the classroom* (7th ed.). Edina, MN: Interaction Book Company.

Kallick, B., & Zmuda, A. (2017). *Students at the center: Personalized learning with Habits of Mind.* Alexandria, VA: ASCD.

Kim, J., & Bryan, J. (2017, April). A first step to a conceptual framework of student and parent empowerment: Exploring relationships between parent empowerment and academic performance in a national sample. *Journal of Counseling & Development, 95,* 168–179.

Konichi, C., & Park, S. (2018, January). Promoting children's healthy social-emotional growth: Dialogue journal. *Journal of Education and Learning, 6*(2), 246–253. doi: 10.5539/jel.v6n2p246

Labaree, D. F. (2011). Citizen and consumers: Changing visions of virtue and opportunity in U.S. education, 1841–1954. In D. Tröhler, T. S. Popkewitz, & D. F. Labaree (Eds.), *Schooling and the making of citizens in the long nineteenth century* (pp. 177–193). New York: Routledge.

Labov, W. (2006, March). *Unendangered dialects, endangered people*. Paper presented at the meeting of the Georgetown University Round Table on Languages and Linguistics (GURT), Washington, DC. Retrieved from http://www.ling.upenn.edu/~wlabov/Papers/UDEP.pdf

Ladner, M. (2018). *12 proverbs that will make you fall in love with the Korean language*. Retrieved from https://theculturetrip.com/asia/south-korea/articles/12-proverbs-that-will-make-you-fall-in-love-with-the-korean-language/

LeMoine, N., & Soto, I. (2016). *Academic language mastery: Culture in context*. Thousand Oaks, CA: Corwin.

Lerner, R. M., Almerigi, J. B., Theokas, C., & Lerner, J. V. (2005). Positive youth development: A view of the issues. *Journal of Early Adolescence, 25*(1), 10–16.

Lewis, S. (2016). *Positive psychology and change: How leadership, collaboration, and appreciative inquiry create transformational results*. West Sussex, UK: Wiley.

Lillard, A. S. (2005). *Montessori: The science behind the genius*. New York: Oxford University Press.

Malala Fund. (2018). Malala's story. Retrieved from https://www.malala.org/malalas-story

Maslow, A. H. (1987). *Motivation and personality* (3rd ed.; R. Frager, J. Fadiman, C. McReynolds, & R. Cox, Eds.). New York: Pearson Longman.

Mayo Clinic. (2019, May 11). Exercise: 7 benefits of regular physical activity. Retrieved from https://www.mayoclinic.org/healthy-lifestyle/fitness/in-depth/exercise/art-20048389

McGonigal, J. (2011). *Reality is broken: Why games makes us better and how they can change the world* [Kindle version]. Retrieved from https://www.amazon.com/Reality-Broken-Games-Better-Change/dp/0143120611/

McGuffey, W. H. (1879). *McGuffey's second eclectic reader*. Retrieved from https://www.gutenberg.org/cache/epub/14668/pg14668.html

McMillan, D. W., & Chavis, D. M. (1986). Sense of community: A definition and theory. *Journal of Community Psychology, 14*(1), 6–23.

Miller, K. (2017, February 8). Does this 83-year-old Supreme Court justice work out harder than you? The jury's out. *Women's Health*. Retrieved from https://www.womenshealthmag.com/fitness/a19956490/ruth-bader-ginsbu/

Minero, E. (2018, March). The architecture of ideal learning environments. Retrieved from https://www.edutopia.org/article/architecture-ideal-learning-environments

Moll, L. C. (2015). Foreword. In J. Allen, J. Beaty, A. Dean, J. Jones, S. Smith Mathew, J. McCreight, . . . & A. M. Simmons (Eds.), *Family dialogue journals: School–home partnerships that support student learning* (p. vii). New York: Teachers College Press.

Montrieux, H., Vanderlinde, R., Schellens, T., & De Marez, L. (2015). Teaching and learning with mobile technology: A qualitative explorative study about the introduction of tablet devices in secondary education. *PLoS ONE, 10*(12), e0144008. doi: 10.1371/journal.pone.0144008

Moon, A., & Neville, A. L. (2017, March 2–4). *Are pre-service teachers prepared for family-teacher relationships*? Paper presented at the American Association of Colleges for Teacher Education (AACTE) 69th Annual Meeting, Tampa, FL.

Moyer, L. (2007, October 24). How the rich raise their kids. *Forbes*. Retrieved from https://www.forbes.com/2007/10/24/millionaires-education-children-biz-cx_lm_1024richkids.html

Murray, L. (2006). *Breaking night: A memoir of forgiveness, survival, and my journey from homeless to Harvard.* New York: Hyperion.

Musu-Gillette, L., Robinson, J., McFarland, J., Kewal Ramani, A., Zhang, A., & Wilkinson-Flicker, S. (2016). Status and trends in the education of racial and ethnic groups 2016 (NCES 2016–007). Washington, DC: U.S. Department of Education, National Center for Education Statistics.

National Center for Education Statistics. (2015). Table 1. Public high school 4-year adjusted cohort graduation rate (ACGR), by race/ethnicity and selected demographics for the United States, the 50 states, and the District of Columbia: School year 2013–14. Retrieved from https://nces.ed.gov/ccd/tables/ACGR_RE_and_characteristics_2013-14.asp

National Center for Education Statistics. (2016). Table 1. Public high school 4-year adjusted cohort graduation rate (ACGR), by race/ethnicity and selected demographics for the United States, the 50 states, and the District of Columbia: School year 2014–15. Retrieved from https://nces.ed.gov/ccd/tables/ACGR_RE_and_characteristics_2014-15.asp

National Center for Education Statistics. (2017). Table 1. Public high school 4-year adjusted cohort graduation rate (ACGR), by race/ethnicity and selected demographic characteristics for the United States, the 50 states, and the District of Columbia: School year 2015–16. Retrieved from https://nces.ed.gov/ccd/tables/ACGR_RE_and_characteristics_2015-16.asp

National Center for Education Statistics. (2019a, May). English language learners in public schools. Retrieved from https://nces.ed.gov/programs/coe/indicator_cgf.asp

National Center for Education Statistics. (2019b, May). The condition of education: Characteristics of postsecondary faculty. Retrieved from https://nces.ed.gov/programs/coe/indicator_csc.asp

National Center for Health Statistics. (2013). The National Survey of Children's Health (NSCH), 2011–2012: The public use data file and documentation. Hyattsville, MD: U.S. Department of Health and Human Services.

Noguera, P. A. (2015). Race, education, and the pursuit of equity in the twenty-first century. In P. A. Noguera, J. C. Pierce, & R. Ahram (Eds.), *Race, equity, and education: Sixty years from Brown* (pp. 3–23). New York: Springer.

Ostroff, W. L. (2012). *Understanding how young children learn: Bringing the science of child development to the classroom.* Alexandria, VA: ASCD.

Pink, D. H. (2009). *Drive: The surprising truth about what motivates us.* New York: Penguin Books.

Porges, S. (2011). *The polyvagal theory: Neurophysiological foundations of emotions, attachment, communication, and self-regulation.* New York: W. W. Norton.

Pozen, R. C. (2013, March 28). The delicate art of giving feedback. *Harvard Business Review.* Retrieved from https://hbr.org/2013/03/the-delicate-art-of-giving-fee

Rach, S., Ufer, S., & Heinze, A. (2012). Learning from errors: Effects of teachers training on students' attitudes towards and their individual use of errors. In Y. T. Tso (Ed.), *Proceedings of the 36th Conference of the International Group for the Psychology of Mathematics Education* (Vol. 3, pp. 329–336). Taipei, Taiwan: PME.

Rivero, V. (2004, April/May). 18 reasons why design matters. Retrieved from http://www.scholastic.com/browse/article.jsp?id=31

Roberts, E. L., Ju, S., & Zhang, D. (2014). Review of practices that promote self-advocacy for students with disabilities. *Journal of Disability Policy Studies, 26,* 209–220.

Rogers, C. (1956). *Client-centered therapy* (3rd ed.). Boston: Houghton Mifflin.

Rogoff, B. (2003). *The cultural nature of human development.* New York: Oxford University Press.

Saint-Jacques, M. C., Turcotte, D., & Pouliot, E. (2009). Adopting a strengths perspective in social work practice with families in difficulty: From theory to practice. *Families in Society, 9,* 454–461. doi: 10.1606/1044-3894.3926

Sardinha, L., Almeida, A. M. P., & Barbas, M. (2017). *The classroom physical space as a learning ecosystem—Bridging approaches: Results from a web survey.* In O. Mealha, M. Divitini, & M. Rehm (Eds.), *Citizen, territory, and technologies: Smart learning contexts and practices: Proceedings of the 2nd International Conference on Smart Learning Ecosystems and Regional Development* (pp. 39–50). Cham, Switzerland: Springer.

Seligman, M. E. P., Rashid, T., & Parks, A. C. (2006). Positive psychotherapy. *American Psychologist, 61*(8), 774–788.

Sharan, S. (1990). *Cooperative learning: Theory and research.* New York: Greenwood Press.

Silverstone, M. (2017, December 19). Classrooms chalk talk: "Row, row, row your boat": Learning and teaching in the round. *Daily Hampshire Gazette.* Retrieved from http://www.gazettenet.com/Chalk-Talk-14410073

Soltero, S. (2016). *Dual language education: Program design and implementation.* Portsmouth, NH: Heinemann.

Sorkin, A. R. (2014, September 5). So Bill Gates has this idea for a high school history class . . . *New York Times Magazine.* Retrieved from https://www.nytimes.com/2014/09/07/magazine/so-bill-gates-has-this-idea-for-a-history-class.html

Southern Education Foundation. (2015). *A new majority: Low income students now a majority in the nation's public schools.* Retrieved from https://files.eric.ed.gov/fulltext/ED555829.pdf

Stanford University. (n.d.). Landmark US cases related to equality of opportunity in K–12 education. Retrieved from https://edeq.stanford.edu/sections/landmark-us-cases-related-equality-opportunity-education

Steele, C. M. (2010). *Whistling Vivaldi and other clues to how stereotypes affect us.* New York: W. W. Norton.

Steele, C. M., & Aronson, J. (1995). Stereotype threat and intellectual test performance of African Americans. *Journal of Personality and Social Psychology, 69,* 797–811.

Stone, S. (2009). Education and social policy. In J. Midgley & M. Livermore (Eds.), *The handbook of social policy* (pp. 381–420). Thousand Oaks, CA: Sage.

Sullivan, K. J. (2017, February 6). U.S. Supreme Court Justice Ruth Bader Ginsburg talks about a meaningful life. Retrieved from https://news.stanford.edu/2017/02/06/supreme-court-associate-justice-ginsburg-talks-meaningful-life/

Suskie, L. (2018). *Assessing student learning: A common sense guide* (3rd ed.). Hoboken, NJ: Jossey-Bass.

U.S. Department of Education. (2016). *The state of racial diversity in the educator workforce.* Washington, DC: Author. Retrieved from https://www2.ed.gov/rschstat/eval/highered /racial-diversity/state-racial-diversity-workforce.pdf

U.S. National Library of Medicine. (2019, May 29). Dehydration. Retrieved from https:// medlineplus.gov/dehydration.html

Walker, J. M. T., & Dotger, B. H. (2012). Because wisdom can't be told: Using comparison of simulated parent-teacher conferences to assess teacher candidates' readiness for family-school partnership. *Journal of Teacher Education, 63*(1), 62–75.

WETA Public Broadcasting. (2019a). Dr. Clemencia Vargas. Retrieved from http://www .colorincolorado.org/dr-clemencia-vargas

WETA Public Broadcasting. (2019b). Video project: How a community school helps ELLs succeed. Retrieved from http://www.colorincolorado.org/videos/classroom-videos/community -schools-and-ells/

Willis, J. (2014, July 18). The neuroscience behind stress and learning. Retrieved from https://www.edutopia.org/blog/neuroscience-behind-stress-and-learning-judy-willis

Wolfram, T. (2019, February 11). Processed foods: What's OK and what to avoid. Retrieved from https://www.eatright.org/food/nutrition/nutrition-facts-and-food-labels/processed -foods-whats-ok-and-what-to-avoid

Yan, H. (2018, May 29). Here's what teachers accomplished with their protests this year. *CNN.* Retrieved from https://www.cnn.com/2018/05/29/us/what-teachers-won-and-lost

Yelland, N. (2006). Changing worlds and new curricula in the knowledge era. *Educational Media International, 43*, 121–131.

Zacarian, D. (2013). *Mastering academic language: A framework for supporting student achievement.* Thousand Oaks, CA: Corwin.

Zacarian, D., Alvarez-Ortiz, L., & Haynes, J. (2017). *Teaching to strengths: Supporting students living with trauma, violence, and chronic stress.* Alexandria, VA: ASCD.

Zacarian, D., & Silverstone, M. A. (2015). *In it together: How student, family, and community partnerships advance engagement and achievement in diverse classrooms.* Thousand Oaks, CA: Corwin.

Zacarian, D., & Silverstone, M. A. (2017, September). Building partnerships through classroom-based events. *Educational Leadership, 75*(1), 12–18.

Zacarian, D., & Soto, I. (2020). *Responsive schooling for culturally and linguistically diverse students.* New York: Norton.

Zull, J. E. (2004, September). The art of changing the brain. *Educational Leadership, 61*(1), 68–72.

Zull, J. E. (2011). *From brain to mind: Using neuroscience to guide change in education.* Sterling, VA: Stylus.

Index

The letter *f* following a page locator denotes a figure.

About the Authors

Debbie Zacarian, EdD, is known for her expertise in strengths-based leadership, instructional practices, and partnerships with culturally and linguistically diverse student and family populations. She has more than three decades of combined experience as a district administrator, university faculty member, and educational service leader. The founder of Zacarian & Associates, she provides sustained policy and practice supports for educators that help them work more successfully with diverse student and family populations. Her authored and coauthored books include *Teaching to Strengths: Supporting Students Living with Trauma, Violence, and Chronic Stress; In It Together: How Student, Family, and Community Partnerships Advance Engagement and Achievement in Diverse Classrooms* (with Michael Silverstone); *Mastering Academic Language: A Framework for Supporting Student Achievement; The Essential Guide for Educating Beginning English Learners; Transforming Schools for English Learners: A Comprehensive Framework for School Leaders;* and *Teaching English Language Learners Across the Content Areas.* Zacarian can be reached at debbie@zacarianconsulting.com.

Michael Silverstone is a veteran primary grades teacher and education writer. After 15 years as a 2nd grade teacher, his interest in intrinsic motivation, mindfulness, and creative expression led him to become a Montessori educator. In 2017, he was selected as an American Montessori Society Emerging Leaders Fellow.

Currently, Silverstone is a staff member of the Montessori Elementary Education Teacher Training Collaborative as well as a lower elementary (ages 6–9) teacher in the Boston area. Silverstone is the author of a number of nonfiction books for children, including *Winona LaDuke: Restoring Land and Culture in Native America* and *Rigoberta Menchu: Defending Human Rights in Guatemala* (Feminist Press at the City University of New York). He and Debbie Zacarian are the coauthors of the book *In It Together: How Student, Family, and Community Partnerships Advance Engagement and Achievement in Diverse Classrooms* and a chapter in *Academic Language in Diverse Classrooms: Mathematics, Grades K–2: Promoting Content and Language Learning.*

Related ASCD Resources

At the time of publication, the following resources were available (ASCD stock numbers in parentheses):

All Learning Is Social and Emotional: Helping Students Develop Essential Skills for the Classroom and Beyond by Nancy Frey, Douglas Fisher, and Dominique Smith (#119033)

Cultural Competence Now: 56 Exercises to Help Educators Understand and Challenge Bias, Racism, and Privilege by Vernita Mayfield (#118043)

The Formative Five: Fostering Grit, Empathy, and Other Success Skills Every Student Needs by Thomas R. Hoerr (#116043)

Self-Regulated Learning for Academic Success: How do I help students manage their thoughts, behaviors, and emotions? (ASCD Arias) by Carrie Germeroth and Crystal Day-Hess (#SF114041)

Students at the Center: Personalized Learning with Habits of Mind by Bena Kallick and Allison Zmuda (#117015)

Teaching Students to Become Self-Determined Learners by Michael L. Wehmeyer and Yong Zhao (#119020)

Teaching to Strengths: Supporting Students Living with Trauma, Violence, and Chronic Stress by Debbie Zacarian, Lourdes Alvarez-Ortiz, and Judie Haynes (#117035)

The Power of Voice in Schools: Listening, Learning, and Leading Together by Russ Quaglia, Kristine Fox, Lisa Lande, and Deborah Young (#120021)

For up-to-date information about ASCD resources, go to www.ascd.org. You can search the complete archives of *Educational Leadership* at www.ascd.org/el.

ASCD myTeachSource®

Download resources from a professional learning platform with hundreds of research-based best practices and tools for your classroom at http://myteachsource.ascd.org/

For more information, send an e-mail to member@ascd.org; call 1-800-933-2723 or 703-578-9600; send a fax to 703-575-5400; or write to Information Services, ASCD, 1703 N. Beauregard St., Alexandria, VA 22311-1714 USA.

THE WHOLE CHILD

The ASCD Whole Child approach is an effort to transition from a focus on narrowly defined academic achievement to one that promotes the long-term development and success of all children. Through this approach, ASCD supports educators, families, community members, and policymakers as they move from a vision about educating the whole child to sustainable, collaborative actions.

Teaching to Empower relates to the **Safe, Engaged, Supported,** and **Challenged** tenets. *For more about the ASCD Whole Child approach, visit* **www.ascd.org/wholechild.**

WHOLE CHILD
TENETS

1 HEALTHY
Each student enters school healthy and learns about and practices a healthy lifestyle.

2 SAFE
Each student learns in an environment that is physically and emotionally safe for students and adults.

3 ENGAGED
Each student is actively engaged in learning and is connected to the school and broader community.

4 SUPPORTED
Each student has access to personalized learning and is supported by qualified, caring adults.

5 CHALLENGED
Each student is challenged academically and prepared for success in college or further study and for employment and participation in a global environment.